The Anniversary

A play

Bill MacIlwraith

Samuel French -
New York – Sydney – Toronto – Hollywood

Rights of Performance by Amateurs are controlled by Samuel French Ltd, 52 Fitzroy Street, London W1P 6JR, and they, or their authorized agents, issue licences to amateurs on payment of a fee. **It is an infringement of the Copyright to give any performance or public reading of the play before the fee has been paid and the licence issued.**

The Royalty Fee indicated below is subject to contract and subject to variation at the sole discretion of Samuel French Ltd.

Basic fee for each and every
    performance by amateurs   Code M
    in the British Isles

ISBN 0 573 11007 7

Please see page iv for further copyright information

THE ANNIVERSARY

This play was first presented by Michael Codron at the Theatre Royal, Brighton, on 28th March, 1966, and subsequently at the Duke of York's Theatre, London, with the following cast:

TOM	*Michael Crawford*
SHIRLEY	*June Ritchie*
HENRY	*James Cossins*
TERRY	*Jack Hedley*
KAREN	*Sheila Hancock*
MUM	*Mona Washbourne*

Directed by PATRICK DROMGOOLE
Designed by HUTCHINSON SCOTT

The action takes place in the living-room of Mum's house, south of London.

ACT ONE   Six p.m. on a Friday evening in November

ACT TWO   Three hours later

ACT THREE   Ten minutes later

No character in this play is intended to portray any specific person, alive or dead.

INTRODUCTION

The central character in *The Anniversary* is dear old Mum, a woman whose possessiveness is a killer. She is thoroughly evil and glories in destroying anything that is good and kind and pure; for not being able to enjoy such feelings herself she is damned if anyone else will. And yet, like the Devil, Mum has an undeniable charm. This woman would never have been drowned as a witch: she would have been crowned Queen.

She has three sons whom she has lacerated with her warped love, and it says something for man's resilience that they are as normal as they are.

Henry has long since succumbed to Mum's dominant personality and settled into a comfortable rut. He has even managed to find an ersatz love that cannot turn round and humiliate him. Terry, although married, still clings to his mother, hoping for a miracle that will never come.

Tom, the youngest son, hates Mum with such venom that he is prepared to sacrifice everyone in order to achieve his aim in life: complete victory over Mum.

Karen, Terry's wife, has fought tenaciously through the years for the body and soul of her husband; but it takes a newcomer, Tom's fiancée Shirley, to be the first to hack through the umbilical cord and free the man she loves.

Shirley and Karen prove that there is hope even where evil appears to be impregnable. There has to be, otherwise we might just as well sit on our personal bomb and blow ourselves into bits of nothing.

I have purposely used a farcical technique, not in order to make the play more palatable to an audience, but in the belief that through laughter a facet of family truth can be accepted without the loss of sanity. Perhaps I'm wrong. You're the judge.

BILL MACILWRAITH

ACT ONE

The living-room of MUM's *house south of London. 6 p.m. on a Friday evening in November.*

The room has been furnished in the contemporary style. There is a sofa C. in front of the glass door leading to the hall and stairs. On the table above the sofa are a telephone, an empty brass vase and an ashtray. In front of the sofa is a low tiled coffee table, on which are a cigarette box, lighter and an ashtray. There is an armchair L. in front of the french windows. Behind an armchair R. is a window overlooking the front garden; below the window is a radiator and D.R. of the window is a glass cabinet crammed with mementoes and souvenirs. On this wall are hung various framed certificates and diplomas. An easy chair D.R. completes the seating arrangements with the exception of a stool in front of the upright piano, which is inside an alcove to the left of the glass door. Lined up on top of the piano are snapshots of children, a large photograph of Dad, a framed certificate and three greetings cards. By the side of the piano is a wastepaper basket. To the right of the door in the U.S. corner is a very modern cocktail cabinet which when opened plays Auld Lang Syne. On top of the cocktail cabinet are a brandy bottle with sufficient drink for two glasses and a table-lamp. There is a standard-lamp to the left of the piano and suspended from the ceiling is a candelabra. On top of the glass cabinet D.R. are a small mirror, a china jug and a back-scratcher. The long draped curtains and the matt-finish paint on the walls are regal in colour.

> *The curtain rises on an empty darkened stage with the hall-light casting a warm glow on the door, which* TOM *throws open as he enters. He is in his early twenties and looks very affluent. His lounge suit is immaculate, his hair stylishly groomed. He is completely relaxed without any trace of self-consciousness. He has a likeable personality and a quick mind. He is an electrician.*

TOM   (*switching on the centre light*) And this is the front-room, living-room, lounge, whatever you like to call it.

(SHIRLEY *enters and looks about her as* TOM *switches on the standard-lamp.* SHIRLEY *is in her late teens with a gentle pretty face and a slim body. She appears to be self-possessed, but nervousness and anxiety are never far from the surface and she is really quite vulnerable. She works in a suburban store and is in love with* TOM.)

SHIRLEY   (*impressed*) Oh, yes; very nice. Very nice indeed.

TOM   (*returning to* SHIRLEY) Not bad, is it?

SHIRLEY   And you and your two brothers built it all by yourselves?

TOM   A good part of it.

SHIRLEY   (*surprised*) You're very clever, aren't you?

TOM   Well, it's our job, ain't it? (*Looking at* SHIRLEY *and giving a roguish chuckle.*) Hide that window.

(*As* SHIRLEY *goes to the window* R. TOM *hurries* L. *and presses one of two switches to the left of the french windows. The curtains automatically close.*)

(*grinning*) How about that, then?

SHIRLEY   (*crossing to the sofa*) Very clever.

(TOM *presses the second switch and the french window curtains come together.*)

TOM   And we did pick out the best of the lads to help us.

SHIRLEY   (*sitting*) Did it take you long?

TOM   (*crossing to the table-lamp on top of the cocktail cabinet*) Longer than we normally take over putting up a house. But then we was going to live in it.

(*He switches on the table-lamp and turns to* SHIRLEY, *but turns back again because the light doesn't come on. He stamps his foot on the floor and this does the trick.* SHIRLEY *glances round and receives a grin from* TOM.)

Here, I've just had a thought.

SHIRLEY   What?

TOM   (*sitting next to her on the sofa*) I haven't had a kiss for five minutes.

(*They go into a clinch.*)

Shall we nip upstairs for a quick one?

SHIRLEY   No, we won't. (*As* TOM *again lunges at her.*) And not here either. We've left cramped sofas behind us. We're engaged.

We're going to be married. We can do it in comfort now; so just contain yourself.

TOM You're right. We've got the whole weekend, haven't we, darling?

SHIRLEY I came here to meet your mum, remember.

TOM I remember.

SHIRLEY You told her we're engaged?

TOM (*with a certain amount of satisfaction*) Tonight, Shirley. I'm telling her tonight.

SHIRLEY (*frowning*) Oh. I was rather hoping you'd already done it.

TOM No. It's got to be tonight.

SHIRLEY I mean, we'd have known where we stood, her and me, right from the start. So she don't know about the baby neither?

TOM (*kindly as he rises*) Tonight, Shirley. She'll know about it all tonight. (*Turning on his way to close the door.*) What with you a couple of months gone and Karen, that's Terry's wife, expecting hers about a month earlier, it's going to be like a pre-natal clinic here.

SHIRLEY Oh, we're not going to be on our own, then?

TOM (*wandering across to the french windows*) No, the whole family will be here. Mum will take us all out for a nosh up, and then back here for the party, and the bonfire, and the fireworks. That's when I mean to tell her about you and me. She'll be in just the right mood to hear it.

SHIRLEY We're having a bit of a party, are we?

TOM Mum always throws a party on her wedding anniversary, Shirley.

SHIRLEY (*puzzled*) Wedding anniversary? I thought your Dad died a few years ago?

TOM (*turning.*) So he did. It's Mum's way of remembering him. Have you got a party piece?

SHIRLEY (*frowning*) A what?

TOM (*crossing to the piano and lifting the lid*) A turn. We all do a turn.

SHIRLEY A turn?

TOM Sing a song, recite, play the piano. (*Vamping with his left hand.*)

SHIRLEY I'm not doing no turn.

TOM Aren't you?

SHIRLEY I'd be too embarrassed.

TOM Mum won't like it.

SHIRLEY (*indignantly*) Then Mum'll have to lump it, won't she?

TOM (*turning*) And you'll tell her, will you?

SHIRLEY She won't get me doing nothing.

TOM She'll be livid.

SHIRLEY (*pointing to the vase behind her*) She can throw that vase at me for all I care.

TOM (*crossing to the sofa*) She probably will.

SHIRLEY Then I'll jolly well throw it back at her.

TOM (*very pleased as he sits next to her*) That's my girl!
(*They kiss until* SHIRLEY *gently pushes him away.*)

SHIRLEY (*quietly*) Will she?

TOM What?

SHIRLEY Throw a vase at me.

TOM I must admit, she don't like not getting her own way. Seems to bring out her femininity.

SHIRLEY I've always wondered why you never asked me home to meet your mum. Now I know.

TOM If I'd brought you back here first time out, I'd never have seen you again. But I knew that once you felt like I felt, you'd give as good as you got.

SHIRLEY (*worried*) I kept thinking perhaps she was a criminal, or couldn't keep off the gin. I never dreamt that you were keeping me away because she might start slinging vases at me.

TOM (*grinning kindly*) I'm sure she won't.

SHIRLEY Have you been joking then?

TOM Depends what you think's funny, don't it?

SHIRLEY Well, I don't think that is. I'm full of nerves as it is, meeting your mum for the first time.

TOM (*rising and taking* SHIRLEY *with him to the glass cabinet*) If you see her going for the vase, Shirley, grab one of these. That'll make her drop it.
(SHIRLEY *looks at the china jug* TOM *is holding.*)

SHIRLEY Why that ugly thing?

TOM (*pretending to be shocked*) Ugly? It's a thing of beauty to

my mum. (*Replacing the china jug.*) Why, Dad might have
kept his shaving water in it. (*Taking hold of the back-
scratcher and using it as a pointer.*) The equivalent of the
crown jewels are inside here, Shirley. Veritable treasures
she's collected over the years. (*Admiringly.*) My first nappy
—Henry's first tooth—Terry's one and only curl—(*Straight-
ening up.*) All beyond price because Mum's got nostalgia-
itis in both legs. (*He lightly touches* SHIRLEY's *stomach
with the back-scratcher.*)

SHIRLEY   Careful.

TOM   (*addressing* SHIRLEY's *stomach*) Sorry, mate.
(*Pointing to the certificates and finishing up by the piano.*)
Same with these certificates. Anyone coming in here would
think : aye, aye; the lads must be Doctors of Philosophy.
But on closer inspection what do they find? Master Henry,
second prize, sack race. Master Thomas, third prize, bible
study. Master Terence, Special Prize for the best loser. I
give you fair warning now, Shirley, you mock all this at
your peril.
(SHIRLEY *crosses upstage.*)

SHIRLEY   (*quietly*) Tom. I've been thinking. I could quite easily go
home after the party.

TOM   (*perturbed as he quickly joins her*) If you love me, you've
got to stay, see it out.

SHIRLEY   But if she turns violent.

TOM   So I'll knock her on the head.

SHIRLEY   (*as* TOM *returns the back-scratcher to the top of the
cabinet*) I think I'd prefer to go if you don't mind.

TOM   (*sincerely, as he takes hold of her*) But I do though. You
see, I look on it as a sort of endurance test, Shirley. If we
can get through this weekend together, we're stuck for
life. Nothing'll ever be as bad again. (*Grinning as a sports
car is heard screeching to a halt outside.*) We're going to
have fun, Shirley. We're going to have fun. (*Crossing to
window R.*) That'll be Henry. (*Looking out as* SHIRLEY
joins him.)

SHIRLEY   (*impressed*) Snazzy sports car, isn't it?

TOM   He can afford it. He hasn't made the long trek down the
aisle yet.

SHIRLEY (*patting her hair into position*) Must be quite a bit of money in building then.

TOM We can't go wrong. Mum buys the land and we help to bung up the houses. With everybody screaming out for property, we're rolling in it. (*Turning to look at her.*) You're marrying into wealth, love.

SHIRLEY (*with a shy giggle as she crosses to the sofa*) Am I really?

TOM Come off it, I've told you often enough.

SHIRLEY (*sitting*) Yer, but I never believed you before.

TOM (*quietly*) But you believe I love you?

SHIRLEY (*simply*) I hope you do, Tom, 'cos I love you.

(TOM *joins her on the sofa and they tenderly kiss.* TOM *then gently brings up his hand to caress her ear, but* SHIRLEY *stops him.*)

No, don't.

TOM But they're lovely.

SHIRLEY Please, Tom.

(TOM *finds her mouth again.* HENRY *enters, carrying a magazine and a large bunch of flowers and wearing sports cap and overalls. He is an inconspicuous man in his late thirties, preferring the shadows to the limelight. He has a neat moustache, a round face and a round body. He is shy, kind, quietly-spoken and resembles a cuddly bear. He halts in his tracks and stares at the couple in surprise before turning to go out.*)

HENRY (*with a smile as he tosses the magazine on to armchair*) Oh, I beg your pardon.

TOM (*as he and* SHIRLEY *break*) It's all right, Henry. No need to creep off. Henry—Shirley. This is Henry.

SHIRLEY (*crossing to shake his hand*) Hello, Henry.

HENRY (*shyly*) Good evening to you.

TOM (*standing behind* SHIRLEY) What do you think, then?

HENRY Think about what?

TOM Shirley

(SHIRLEY *shyly crosses to the sofa where she sits.*)

HENRY Oh, very nice. Very nice. (*Quietly in* TOM's *ear.*) You know Mum will be here shortly. (*He places the flowers on the table above the sofa.*)

TOM So what?

HENRY Well, you know, if you want to say cheerio to Shirley; well, that's all right, ain't it?

TOM (*sitting next to* SHIRLEY) But Shirley's staying, Henry.

HENRY Staying?

TOM For the weekend. In the guest-room.

HENRY Oh. (*Crossing to the door and then turning.*) Mum didn't say.

TOM (*grinning*) Mum doesn't know.

(HENRY *crosses to the glass cabinet* D.R. *and adjusts the china jug.*)

SHIRLEY (*frowning*) Doesn't know?

TOM I'm giving her a surprise.

SHIRLEY (*staring at* TOM) But I thought she'd invited me.

TOM I never told you that.

SHIRLEY But this means she's being imposed upon.

TOM I don't see why?

SHIRLEY What, having someone stay and not knowing about it?

HENRY (*moving in a few paces*) Shirley's right. You should have told Mum.

SHIRLEY (*anxiously to* HENRY *as she rises*) Do you think I ought to go?

HENRY (*kindly*) Yes, I do really.

TOM (*making her sit*) She's not leaving. You're not leaving, Shirley.

HENRY (*appealing to* TOM) But there's no need for her to stay, Tom. You'll have what you're after, anyway. I mean, the sparks are going to fly when Terry ups and tells her about himself.

SHIRLEY Tells her what?

HENRY It's a family matter, Shirley.

TOM But Shirley's one of the family, Henry. (*Slipping an arm round her waist.*) We're engaged, aren't we, darling?

SHIRLEY We're picking up the ring tomorrow.

HENRY (*after a little cough*) Yer, well, I think I'll go and get changed. (*A shade too casually as he crosses to the door and opens it.*) Do you think perhaps I could see you for a moment on your own, Tom?

TOM (*rising and crossing to* HENRY) No, Henry.

HENRY (*as* TOM *wanders to above the sofa*) But there's something I want to say to you, Tom.

TOM Then say it, Henry.

HENRY In private.

(SHIRLEY *takes a mirror from her handbag and looks at herself.*)

TOM Spit it out, mate.

(HENRY *hesitates before closing the door and taking a few paces into the room.*)

HENRY I just want to know if—well, if you, if you're fond of her.

TOM (*sincerely*) I'm in love with her.

(SHIRLEY *registers pleasure as she puts away her mirror.*)

HENRY It's not a trick?

TOM (*indignantly as he crosses* D.L.) Why should it be a trick?

HENRY Then for her sake, you ought to wait before telling Mum.

TOM She's going to be told tonight. (*He spreadeagles himself in the chair* D.R.)

HENRY But you're asking too much from Shirley.

SHIRLEY (*glancing at* TOM) You can't ask too much from someone who loves you.

TOM (*to* HENRY) D'you hear that? Now isn't that nice? Don't you think that's nice?

(*Three children are heard screaming their way upstairs and calling for 'Uncle Henry'.*)

SHIRLEY (*surprised*) Who's arrived?

TOM At a rough guess I'd say about three of Terry's kids.

SHIRLEY How many's he got then?

TOM Five, and one on the way.

HENRY (*beaming*) Hear the little blighters? They're calling for me.

TOM Yer, they love their Uncle Henry, don't they, Henry?

TERRY (*off*) Shut up! I said be quiet! And if you go into Nannie's room, I'll thump you! (*As he runs upstairs.*) I said not into Nannie's room!

HENRY (*as the children's voices fade*) Better go to them before they get a walloping.

TOM (*quickly crossing upstage to join* HENRY) Bring 'em in here, Henry. Introduce them to Shirley.

HENRY (*his smile disappearing*) You know they're not allowed.

SHIRLEY Not allowed?

HENRY (*a shade uncomfortable*) Mum put it out of bounds after
       they'd done a pile of damage.

TOM   (*wandering down to above sofa*) One of them broke an
       egg-cup, Shirley.

HENRY It had a great sentimental value to Mum.
       (HENRY *opens the door and* TERRY *enters carrying a bunch
       of flowers. He is a thin, fairly tall man of thirty-four, with
       a long, rather woebegone face.* SHIRLEY *rises and eases
       L.*)

TERRY Where's that loud-mouthed, skinny, no good ignorant lazy
       lout— (*Seeing* SHIRLEY.) Who are you?

SHIRLEY (*rather taken aback*) Shirley.
       (TERRY *gazes at her before turning his attention on* TOM,
       who is grinning away. SHIRLEY *sits in armchair D.L.*)

TERRY (*as* TOM *joins him*) You left a live cable dangling from the
       loft of plot seven. I could have been electrocuted.

TOM   Wasn't my fault. I couldn't find no conduit. Anyway, I
       think it's a dead liberty calling us in for repairs. After all,
       they only moved into the house last week. Everything
       would have righted itself.

TERRY If everyone did their work properly, there'd be no repairs
       to do.

TOM   Hark at you! Just hark at you. Who built a broom cup-
       board right behind the door so that you had to walk into
       the kitchen sideways?
       (*He walks sideways to armchair* R. *where he sits.*)

TERRY (*mumbling*) Everyone can make a mistake now and again.
       I'm no exception.

TOM   You are, mate, because you never stop making them.
       (TERRY *turns and points the flowers at* SHIRLEY.)

HENRY (*quickly*) Did you find time to look at the staircase of plot
       twelve, Terry?

TERRY (*sitting on right arm of sofa*) I had to, didn't I? They was
       moving in this afternoon.

HENRY Was it much away from the wall?

TERRY About an inch.

TOM   It was only half an inch when I noticed it last night.
       (*Grinning.*) They ought to be delighted. They're getting a
       moving staircase for nothing.

TERRY (*grumbling*) I had to work right through the lunch-hour on it. No wonder I got an ulcer.

HENRY How did you get rid of the gap?

TERRY Wood filler! Got through tubes of the stuff.

CHILDREN'S VOICES–(*in unison*) Uncle Henry!

HENRY (*smiling and calling out*) Coming!

TERRY (*rising and going to above sofa*) Hold on. (*Gazing at* SHIRLEY) So what's this one doing here, then?

HENRY They're engaged. Terry. (*Soothingly.*) But they are in love. They are in love, Terry.

(HENRY *goes out and a cheer goes up from the children.*)

TERRY (*to* TOM, *as he carefully places the flowers on the table*) You git!

TOM (*agreeably*) I hope you've noticed, Shirley; we're a very polite family.

(TERRY *looks at* SHIRLEY *and suddenly smiles as he walks D.S. and sits on the edge of the coffee table.*)

TERRY You're not engaged.

TOM We are, you know.

TERRY (*sympathetically*) He's put you up to this, hasn't he?

SHIRLEY (*puzzled*) I beg your pardon?

TERRY How much is he paying you?

SHIRLEY What?

TERRY To do this act.

SHIRLEY (*bewildered*) What act?

TERRY Kidding everyone you're engaged to him.

SHIRLEY It's no act. We're going to get married.

TERRY I tell you it's an act.

SHIRLEY It's not.

TERRY It is.

SHIRLEY (*becoming angry*) Look, I should know, shouldn't I?

TOM (*grinning*) It's no good, Shirley. His brain's radioactive. That's why it's surrounded by lead, so's nothing will get in or out.

TERRY (*taking out a wad of notes*) Look, I'm not wasting any more time. I'll give you fifty quid to clear off.

SHIRLEY (*rising and going to* TOM *for protection*) I'm not going no-where. I'm staying. Tom's invited me to stay.

TOM (*rising and crossing to* TERRY) For the weekend, Terry.

TERRY (*turning round*) You conniving two-faced little runt. Well, you're not springing it on Mum tonight.

TOM (*grinning*) I've got news for you.

TERRY Not tonight!

TOM Tonight.

TERRY (*seething*) God, I've got a good mind to fling you straight through that door!

TOM (*unabashed*) Wouldn't hurt, mate, it's one of your doors: (*Crossing to door.*) papier maché, a pot of glue and matches.

(KAREN *enters carrying flowers, handbag and basket containing toys and a pair of shoes. She is in her early thirties, plumpish, and has a bright personality and an assured manner. Leaving the door open, she places flowers and handbag on the table above the sofa and the basket on the floor.* TERRY *wanders upstage, while* TOM *joins* SHIRLEY.)

KAREN (*pleasantly*) The last time in this house. It's like paying off a mortgage. (*Noticing* SHIRLEY *and glancing at* TERRY.)

TERRY He says he's engaged to her.

SHIRLEY (*hotly*) I've got a handle, just like you, you know.

TERRY (*as* KAREN *slips off her coat and leaves it on R. arm of sofa*) Henry thinks they're in love.

SHIRLEY We are in love!

(KAREN *grins and crosses to* TOM *whom she kisses.*)

KAREN Congratulations, Tom. (*She returns to table.*)

TOM It's on the level, Karen.

KAREN (*surprised*) Is it?

TOM Definitely.

(KAREN *gazes at him for a moment and then chuckles.*)

KAREN Even better. (*She takes her shoes from the basket.*)

TOM (*grinning*) Yes, I thought it would please your sense of humour.

TERRY Well, I don't believe it.

KAREN I do. It had to happen some time; why not now?

TOM And you're all for it, aren't you?

KAREN Not arf. I'll be needing reinforcements this evening. (*Kindly to* SHIRLEY.) What's your name, love?

SHIRLEY Shirley.

KAREN (*with a quick kiss on her cheek*) Congratulations, Shirley.

(*Crossing to sofa.*) Yer, well, this is going to be another one in the eye for the old bag, ain't it? (*Sitting.*) I presume she don't know yet.

SHIRLEY Tom's telling her tonight.

(KAREN *chortles, as* SHIRLEY *smiles at* TOM *before crossing D.R. where she sits.* KAREN *quickly removes her boots and slips on the shoes.*)

TERRY (*to* TOM) Well, I'm having my say first, I'm telling her about me first. Then you can detonate your floozie in her face. But wait till Karen and me are out of the way.

KAREN No, I want to be here when it happens. You tell her as soon as I get back from dumping the kids.

(*A car pulls up outside, and* TOM *wanders over to the window.*)

TOM I'll pick my moment.

KAREN (*grinning*) I bet you will.

SHIRLEY Aren't the children staying for the party?

KAREN What? She can't stand the sight of 'em. No, she'll give them their anniversary present each, and then I'll quickly whisk 'em back home. Come to think of it, they're a bit quiet, aren't they?

TERRY They're with Henry.

KAREN (*frowning*) Oh, are they? (*Rising and placing her boots in the basket.*) Nip up and see that they're all right, Terry.

TERRY Why shouldn't they be all right?

KAREN You know how I feel about Henry.

TERRY He's harmless.

KAREN Is he?

(*The slam of the front door is heard.*)

TOM (*rubbing his hands as he comes away from the window*) Here she is, the fairy godmother. She's arrived.

(KAREN *immediately sits on arm of chair R. and picks up the magazine.* SHIRLEY *nervously rises.*)

KAREN (*gesturing*) Sit down.

SHIRLEY Just thought I'd tidy up a bit, put on a face.

KAREN Whatever face you put on would be wrong, so sit down.

(MUM *enters. She is in her late fifties and average in height and weight. She has a slight stoop, a great deal of nervous energy and there is a menacing quality about her that*

*spells danger to anyone contemplating crossing her. She
also has an inherent charm, and this charm prevents her
more obnoxious remarks from leaving a taste.*

*She is wearing a spy glass at the end of a length of ribbon
and a mink coat which is open revealing an attractive
dress).*

MUM (*pleasantly*) Every time your kids come and visit me,
Karen, they bring half the garden with them. (*Removing
her gloves as she crosses to the table above the sofa.*)
There's mud all up the stairs.

KAREN (*unperturbed*) Strange, I made them take their shoes and
socks off before they came in.

MUM Then all I can say is, it's high time you washed their feet.
(*Gazing down at the flowers.*) So when am I being buried?
(KAREN *rises.*)

TERRY ⎫
TOM ⎬ (*together—tonelessly*) Happy anniversary, Mum.
KAREN ⎭

MUM (*beaming*) Ah, you've remembered. I wondered if you
would.

KAREN Didn't you get the card we sent you, then?

TOM Of course she did.

MUM (*sweetly to* SHIRLEY) Hello, dear.

SHIRLEY (*nervously*) Hello.

MUM (*surveying her from right of sofa*) You're not one of
Karen's, are you?

KAREN (*pleasantly*) How can she be one of mine, Mum? She don't
look like Terry, and all the rest do, don't they?

MUM Ah, but you could have had her before you met Terry.
(MUM *chuckles and* KAREN *chuckles in reply before pulling
a face behind* MUM's *back.*) Friend of yours, my little
Tommy Tucker?

TOM (*taking* SHIRLEY's *hand and making her rise*) Shirley, this
is my mum.

(SHIRLEY *holds out her hand, which* MUM *ignores.*)

MUM And would you like her to stay, Tommy?

TOM She is staying, Mum.

MUM That's what I said, dear. Would you like her to stay?

TOM Yes.

MUM (*talking to her as if she were a four-year-old*) Would you like to stay, Shirley?

SHIRLEY Er, thank you.

(MUM *holds out her hand and* SHIRLEY *quickly shakes it.*)

MUM We'll see you get home before your mummy starts worrying about you.

(MUM *brings up her spy glass and gazes at* KAREN's *coat draped over the arm of the sofa.* TERRY *hurriedly picks it up and places it on the piano stool.* MUM *sits on the sofa while* SHIRLEY *and* TOM *exchange glances.* SHIRLEY *then sits D.R.*)

And now, where are my grandchildren?

TERRY Upstairs.

MUM (*surprised*) Why aren't the little darlings playing in here?

TOM We didn't want them to break another egg-cup.

MUM (*with a roguish chuckle as she eyes* TOM) You sadist, you. (*Frowning as she glances at* KAREN.) They're not thieving around in my room, are they, Karen?

KAREN They're with their Uncle Henry.

MUM (*melting*) Then no wonder they're behaving themselves. He knows how to handle children, does Henry. No brute force with him. It's all done with gentleness and the soothing hand, Shirley.

(KAREN *takes exception to* MUM's *remark, picks up her basket and coat and goes into the hall with them.*)

I do hope he'll have some of his own soon. He deserves to.

(TERRY *sits on left arm of sofa.*)

SHIRLEY Oh, I thought he wasn't married.

MUM (*amused*) I don't know, you youngsters: anyone over twenty, and he's ready for burning. (*She gazes at* SHIRLEY *for a moment or two before continuing, kindly, almost sadly*) You can't hide it, I'm afraid, Shirley.

SHIRLEY (*surprised*) Hide what?

MUM A tossed-off remark like that gives it away.

(KAREN *closes the door as she re-enters and wanders over to the left of* TERRY. *They give each other a smile of encouragement.*)

SHIRLEY Gives what away?

MUM How you was brought up, dear. You see, with the aristocracy, thirty-six is thought the correct age for a man to marry.

KAREN But Henry's no longer thirty-six, Mum.

MUM He happens to be waiting for his true love, Karen. He's not like some who'll marry the first bint who winks him over to the nearest bed; eh, Terry? We know, don't we? (TERRY *grins and glances up at* KAREN *who gives his arm a slap with her hand.* TERRY's *grin fades.*)

No, he's got ideals, has Henry. Of course his difficulty, Shirley, is trying to stop greedy skinny gold-diggers from slipping inside his wallet. But he always manages to smell them out, flick them off. I don't know how, but he does. How did you get on with him, Shirley; all right?

SHIRLEY All right.

MUM Yes, he's very polite always. He'd have been an ambassador by now if he'd gone into the diplomatic. (*Sitting in armchair* R.)

TOM That's perfectly true, Shirley. It took him ages when he left elementary school at fourteen deciding between the diplomatic and the building trade.

MUM (*annoyed*) Don't belittle your brother, Tommy.

TOM I'm not belittling him——

MUM He's the head of the house. He deserves your respect. He's the one who'd have got the title, not you. (*With her roguish look.*) Oh, you know how to pull me down, don't you, you little ravisher. (*Opening her handbag.*) I suppose I'd better go and take the brats their presents.

TERRY You shouldn't have bothered, Mum.

MUM But I like doing it. I like to see their little faces light up.

KAREN What have you brought them, Mum?

MUM Notice, Shirley, there's no subtleties with Karen. Straight to the basic essential. What have you brought them? If you want to know, I'm giving them the money. (*She opens her handbag and takes out an envelope.*)

KAREN Good idea. Let them buy what they want.

MUM Thank you for your advice, but I've already bought it. I've had the money put into unit trusts where no one can get her hands on it.

(MUM *beams at* KAREN *who returns the beam as she*

wanders above the sofa towards TOM, *who is playfully wagging a finger at her.*)
Really, I don't honestly know what you're complaining about, Karen. After all, you get a nice lot of pin money every month out of child allowance.

KAREN (*pleasantly*) I didn't know I was complaining, Mum.

MUM You can't understand why I just don't give you the money to put into the post-office, so called.

KAREN Can't I, Mum?

MUM I'm just looking after their interest, Karen, that's all. Is that so very wrong?

KAREN It's very laudable, Mum.

MUM So what are you so raving jealous about?

KAREN Your complexion, Mum. I always wanted a complexion like you've got.

(MUM *gazes at* KAREN *and then gives a little laugh.*)

MUM Soap and water, dear. Soap and water. (*Patting her face.*) And lots of patting all over. (*Rising and going upstage.*) Are the children staying?

(SHIRLEY *and* TERRY *rise while* KAREN *eases* R.)

TERRY No, Mum.

MUM (*surprised*) Why ever not?

KAREN Would you like them to stay, Mum?

MUM (*crestfallen*) But who's going to look after them?

KAREN My mother.

MUM (*pursing her lips*) Oh, I see. You've already arranged it between yourselves, have you? Five minutes with me, five hours with her. If you can pinch back your trousers, Terry, I'd like to see my grandchildren occasionally.

TERRY They're upstairs waiting for you.

MUM (*grinning*) Waiting to see what I've brought them, you mean. (*Opening the door.*) Don't forget, I've had three chicks of my own. (*Turning.*) Only three, I grant you, Karen. But then natural good manners told me when to put the plug in.

(MUM *closes the door as she goes out.* KAREN *and* TERRY *sit on the sofa and relax while* SHIRLEY *sits* D.R. KAREN *takes a cigarette, which* TERRY *lights for her.*)

TOM Well, do you think she's realised?

KAREN What?

TOM That I'm quite serious about Shirley.

KAREN She's no doubt wondering what Shirley's doing up your sleeve.

TOM So why didn't she ask me?

TERRY Why should she, when she can find it all out from Henry?

TOM (*worried as he rises and wanders upstage*) Damn, I'd forgotten about him. (*Halting.*) But he won't tell her. He's not one for stirring it. (*Wandering D.R.*) No, he won't tell her.

KAREN If you wanted to keep the engagement secret till after Mum had proposed the toast, you should have hidden Shirley up the chimney. That's the only way you'd have stopped Mum's brain from racing to a hundred thousand conclusions.

SHIRLEY That crack about skinny gold-diggers was meant for me, you know.

KAREN How did you find your future in-law?

SHIRLEY (*crossing to* KAREN) It's quite nerve-racking really, ain't it?

KAREN I always leave here with a screaming headache, and my whole body shaking with murder and hate. But not for long now. (*Slipping an arm through* TERRY's.) We'll soon be out of it, won't we, Terry?

TERRY (*nodding and smiling*) Yer.

SHIRLEY Where you going, then?

KAREN Canada. Way up north.

TOM (*as* SHIRLEY *returns to chair* D.R.) Mum can't stand the cold.

TERRY Do you think she knows about us, too?

KAREN She must know something's up, because you've been going round for the past couple of months like a driver who's just knocked down a policeman on a zebra crossing. Don't worry, she's been burrowing about, sniffing around, I bet.

TERRY Make it a lot easier if she does know.

TOM Why?

TERRY My trouble is I don't like hurting her.

TOM (*crossing to sofa*) Your trouble is you've always let her play the tune on your guts.

KAREN (*defending* TERRY) Leave off now. Terry's got feelings. He's the sensitive one among us.

TOM *(lifting his eyes to the ceiling with amused sarcasm as he swings upstage)* Gawd save us!

SHIRLEY *(not to be outdone)* Tom's very sensitive too, I've found. (TOM, KAREN *and* TERRY *turn to look at her.*)

KAREN I'm not talking about being ticklish in the long grass, Shirley.

TOM *(frowning)* I am sensitive.

TERRY You're not, otherwise you wouldn't have brought your floozie here tonight. This is Mum's night.

TOM So when are you going to tell Mum you're emigrating?

TERRY I've got to give her a week's notice, haven't I?

TOM You could have told her yesterday or last week.

TERRY I didn't want to upset her.

TOM But you're going to upset her tonight.

TERRY Because I've got to give her a week's notice.

TOM So how does that make you more sensitive than me?

KAREN That proves you're not sensitive, otherwise you'd know.

SHIRLEY *(rising)* Excuse me, but I don't see how your husband is all that sensitive if he can turn round twice inside half an hour and call me a floozie. Because even if I am, I don't like to be told it.

TOM Good for you, Shirley. Don't you be sat on by these two. With their weight you'd go straight through the floorboards.

TERRY Who started this stupid argument anyway?

TOM You must have done if it's stupid.

KAREN It wasn't Terry, it was me. And it wasn't an argument, it was a fact. Terry's the sensitive one of the family, otherwise why wouldn't he have cleared out years ago?

TERRY Drop it, Karen.

KAREN I'm sorry, but I'm not sitting here listening to you being ridiculed.

TOM Who's ridiculing him?

KAREN Don't be rude, Tom!

SHIRLEY You were ridiculing Tom!

TERRY *(rising and crossing to french windows)* Shut up, the lot of you! Like a pack of wolves tearing into nothing. It's this house. Five minutes inside it and everyone gets the screaming abdabs.

KAREN (*quietly*) He's right, you know.

TOM (*wandering to below piano*) Yes, he is. Makes you want to itch, draw blood. Ought to be pulled down. (*Grinning.*) That's a thought, isn't it? Pour petrol over it, start a fire.

KAREN (*grinning expectantly*) Where's Mum, Tom? Where's Mum?

TOM I gave her some sleeping tablets. She's in bed snoring away, her teeth grinning in a glass of water. And the flames are licking her legs, (*Touching* TERRY'*s knees before crossing to* SHIRLEY.) and she thinks old Dad's returned.
(TOM *and* KAREN *find this very amusing, but not* SHIRLEY. *She turns and sits* D.R.)

SHIRLEY I've never heard you talking like that before.

TOM You've never seen me with my Mum before. The times she's been perfectly murdered.

TERRY Belt up, you ungrateful nit.

SHIRLEY You murder your Mum?

TOM At least once a week.

SHIRLEY But that's horrible. I mean she's your Mum.
(HENRY *enters. He is now wearing a lounge suit.*)

HENRY She wants to know who's taking the kids home.

TOM (*impatiently*) Did you tell her about the engagement?

HENRY (*surprised*) But you told her, didn't you?

TOM (*furiously*) You fat ponce! I didn't want her to find out.

HENRY But she knew. She come up and said, 'So when's the wedding?' Just like that.

TOM (*ramming fist into palm as he slowly crosses to the window*) Spoilt! My big dramatic moment. Spoilt! Something I've really been looking forward to so much—spoilt!

TERRY (*crossing to L. of sofa*) How did she take it?

HENRY (*picking up the magazine from armchair and crossing below the sofa*) Seemed all excited, especially when I said that he really loved her. (*Sitting on chair D.L.*)

KAREN (*happily*) Good. Reaction should be setting in about now.

HENRY The children are ready to leave when you are.

TERRY I suppose you want to stay, Karen?

KAREN Yes, please!
(TERRY *goes out.*)

It's not often I get a ringside seat. I'm usually inside the ring, on the ropes. I can't miss this.

TOM *(aggrieved)* And I had it all sorted out; I was going to frizzle her with it. And now it's her who's got the hand on the switch. *(Sitting in armchair R.)* How the hell does she manage it?

(TERRY re-enters.)

TERRY You've got to take 'em home, love.

KAREN Why not you?

TERRY *(sitting)* She's got something to tell me.

KAREN *(suspiciously)* What is it?

TERRY She says it's a surprise.

KAREN She can tell you later.

TERRY She says it can't wait. *(He wanders to above sofa.)*

SHIRLEY *(to KAREN in some agitation)* Please! Don't go.

TOM *(surprised)* Why? What's the matter with you then?

SHIRLEY *(to TOM)* I don't want to be left alone with your Mum.

TOM Get out of it, I'm here, aren't I?

KAREN I know how she feels. When you're preparing for battle, you want your own sex around you. Don't worry, love. I'm not leaving. She's up to something and she wants me out of the way.

(MUM enters, without her mink coat.)

MUM Hurry, Karen, before they wreck Terry's car. *(Crossing to the sofa.)* I find them all very lovely but quite exhausting. *(She looks at KAREN who rises in order that MUM may sit. KAREN then decides to sit at the other end of the sofa. This does not please MUM.)* Do you want them to drive off without you, dear, because that's what they'll do if you don't move yourself.

KAREN *(with a rueful smile)* I can't, Mum, I'm afraid. The little perisher's making me feel quite faint.

MUM Nonsense. It's not big enough yet. Unless of course you've got an ugly great bear in there.

KAREN *(smiling)* Well, at least there'll be someone coming along who'll look like me; eh, Mum?

MUM *(returning the smile)* You never cease to amaze me, Karen. Why do you want every child to look like you? Let them have some chance in life, for God's sake.

TERRY Look, what about the kids? Who's taking them home?

MUM (*concerned*) Like poor little orphans—nobody wanting to own them. But if they was rabbits or cats, you'd all be jumping out of the window in your eagerness to comfort them.

TERRY I was all ready to take 'em home, Mum.

MUM (*pursing her lips*) It's not convenient, Terry.

HENRY (*rising*) Shall I take them home, then?

(MUM *stretches out her arms towards* HENRY *and gazes at him in adoration.*)

MUM Why is it you always have to fall back on my Henry to help you out of your difficulties? You're a real crusader, Henry, and the world's better for having you around. (*To* SHIRLEY.) There are times, Shirley, when I'm sorry we aren't Roman Catholics. Henry would have made a lovely Pope. Henry the Humble.

(HENRY *crosses below the sofa and turns upstage.*)

(*To* HENRY.) But no mucking about. Come straight home. It'll soon be time to leave for the restaurant.

(HENRY *goes into the hall for his coat.*)

(*To* SHIRLEY.) We're having prawn cocktails to start off with, Shirley. But it's not a drink, dear; so use the spoon provided.

HENRY (*from the doorway as he slips on his coat*) Can I buy them some ice-cream, Karen?

MUM He's generous to a fault, is my eldest.

KAREN No, thank you, Henry. They're being rationed to one a day, and they've had their quota.

MUM (*staring at* KAREN) What are you preparing them for: the next war? Do they have to sleep down the tube twice a week, and wear gas-masks round the house? Rationing! Really Karen, I know you won't mind me saying this, but you're a very hard mother.

KAREN That's how I want their teeth to be, Mum. Good and hard.

MUM Now don't put words into my mouth. I never said good. I don't think you are a good mother, though it's certainly not my place to say it.

KAREN (*with resigned patience*) Then why say it, Mum?

MUM Because there are some things that have to be said if we're going to get on with each other. Live and let live, Karen.

KAREN (*rising and going to the french windows*) Yes, Mum. I agree.

MUM So, tell the kids the ice-cream's from their Nannie, Henry.
(KAREN *swings round angrily and* MUM *smiles brightly at her.* KAREN *then sits D.L.*)

TERRY (*following* HENRY *into the hall*) Here, you'd better take the car keys. And I don't want no trouble from the police about lights, so keep them on if you park outside the house.

SHIRLEY (*as* TERRY *re-enters*) Ice-cream is very bad for teeth.
(*There is silence while* MUM *slowly turns to gaze at* SHIRLEY).

MUM Oh, she's awake, is she? (*With a brittle smile and an underlying edge as she pats the side of the sofa.*) Come over here, dear. Sit beside me. Let me get a good look at you.
(SHIRLEY *glances at* TOM *before rising, and crosses to the sofa where she sits.* MUM *gazes at her.*)
His tastes seem to be changing. He used to like to feel a lot of flesh. I'm afraid you wouldn't fetch much in Sainsbury's. Is she sleeping in the guest-room, Tommy?

TOM Yer. That's right, Mum.

MUM (*to* SHIRLEY) I keep meaning to get a new bed; one that don't creak. I never get a good night's sleep, Shirley, when Tom has his guests to stay. All that creaking. But of course I never mention it. After all, he's been gifted with all this wonderful energy. It's got to be used up somehow. And I don't like embarrassing the girls.

TOM (*crossing to* MUM) It won't work, Mum. Shirley's not going to take a scrap of notice of your ravings; so, go on, you enjoy yourself, have fun.

SHIRLEY (*taking the plunge*) We're going to get married.

MUM (*kindly and without a pause*) Will it be a white wedding, dear?

SHIRLEY (*astonished at* MUM's *reaction*) Er, yes. Yes, it will.

MUM You'll look radiant in white. And how many bridesmaids: two?
(SHIRLEY *nods.*)
I bet they'll be in yellow. And they'll each carry a bouquet

and you'll carry a prayer book. And the bells will ring, ting-a-ling-a-ling, and you'll be so happy, dear; and we'll all be happy for you. And I promise we'll be very sympathetic when Tom fails to turn up.

(TOM *is about to make a retort but* TERRY *comes down and tugs at his sleeve. Without another word* TOM *crosses to R.*)

TERRY (*with bored impatience*) Isn't it about time we changed the subject?

MUM (*gaily*) Just listen to Terry! Honestly, you're still the same little boy hating it when the spotlight isn't on you. (*Cooing to him.*) So haven't we noticed you for two minutes? Did you think you'd been forgotten?

(KAREN *rises and crosses to above the sofa where she takes a cigarette from her handbag.*)

(*Seriously, as she leans slightly back to get a better view.*) I don't think I've ever seen such a strong disciplined face in my life; and I'm not just saying that, Shirley love, because he happens to be my son. It seems to be hewn out of granite. It's the face of a man who's suffered and has come through it all. Am I right, Karen?

(*An embarrassed* TERRY *shuffles over to R.*)

KAREN I should say he's still suffering, wouldn't you, Mum?

MUM (*kindly*) You think you've failed him, do you, dear? Well, at least you're honest about it.

(*The phone rings and* MUM *stretches out an arm to take it.*) Pilgrim 8822. Yes? (*Pause.*) Speaking. (*Amazed.*) No! Oh, that's very bad, isn't it? (*Pause.*) Well, it's almost criminal negligence, isn't it? But don't you worry, I'll send one of my sons over to blow them up first thing in the morning. Goodbye. (*As she replaces the receiver.*) Remind Henry to go to the house on Fenton Street. We forgot to put in the damp course. (*Not at all concerned.*) I don't know, we seem to be having lots of complaints lately.

TERRY I've told you why. It's that clause you got inserted in all contracts. (*Wandering above the sofa.*) I mean, it's ridiculous. Fifty quid off the price for every day we're behind schedule!

MUM That's what's known as a good selling point. Besides, the customer has a right to know when he can move in.

TERRY   Working like slaves just to make sure we're not fined. (*Moving further L.*) And you won't bring in extra staff to help out, will you?

MUM   We've got enough layabouts living off us. Bring in any more, and our standards would suffer.

TOM   That would be quite impossible.

TERRY   (*moving to L. of sofa*) We just can't keep up the pace, Mum. It's crippling us.

KAREN   Yes.

MUM   (*turning and smiling politely at* SHIRLEY) Shirley dear, would you mind going and sitting elsewhere. I find B.O. offensive.

SHIRLEY (*furiously, as she rises*) I haven't got B.O!

TOM   (*quickly*) Shirley!
       (SHIRLEY *crosses to* TOM *who gives her a comforting squeeze as he leads her to the chair D.R. and gently sits her down.* MUM *pats the sofa and* TERRY *sits.*)

MUM   Anyway, Terry, you won't be feeling like this when you move.
       (TERRY *and* KAREN *exchange glances as he half rises in alarm.*)
       (*Smiling.*) I thought that would surprise you. Yes, I've bought you a new house.

KAREN   (*suspiciously*) Why?

MUM   I'm sure some people would be overcome with gratitude, Karen, at such news. But not you, dear. You ask why, as if I'm doing it out of spite. You've had it too easy, Karen. (*To* SHIRLEY.) You won't be getting no backhanders from me, Shirley.

SHIRLEY (*still seething*) I don't want no backhanders from you.

MUM   (*to* TERRY *with a sad smile*) See?

TERRY   (*a shade worried*) You haven't paid for it, have you, Mum?

MUM   Next week. Twelve thousand quid.

TOM   (*crossing to R. of sofa*) Twelve thousand quid? Where's the contract then, Mum?

MUM   With the solicitors. (*Casually, as she shrugs her shoulders.*) Of course if you don't want it, for one reason or another, you'd better tell me now.

TOM   Watch her, Terry. She's fishing.

KAREN   (*impatiently*) Shut up, Tom.

(TOM *wanders round to the piano*.)

TERRY   (*overwhelmed*) Twelve thousand quid. (*Glancing at* KAREN.)
What about that, eh, Karen? (*Innocently, to* MUM.) Why,
Mum? Why do you want to give us a house?

MUM   You haven't been looking yourself lately, son. Gone very
quiet, introspective.

TOM   (*singing it out*) She's fishing. (*Slowly returning to R. of
sofa*.)

MUM   I put it down to being so cramped in the house you're in
at the moment, always falling over the kids. So I thought a
change of environment might help. Will you take it in
the spirit with which it is being offered, God bless you,
son?

TERRY   (*frowning as he mumbles his gratitude*) It's very kind of
you, Mum. Very kind.

TOM   (*sitting on R. arm of sofa*) Ask to see the contract, Terry.

MUM   (*savagely, as she flings a look at* TOM) I had you summed
up when you poked your head out. I said: This one's a
Thomas. And I was right, right, right!

(*A subdued* TOM *returns to the armchair and sits*.)

(*Affectionately to* TERRY.) Well, son? Are you going to
please your old Mum on her anniversary?

TERRY   (*uncomfortably*) Very kind indeed.

MUM   Will you accept it with my love?

KAREN   (*impatiently*) Tell her, Terry.

MUM   (*kindly*) Tell me what, Terry?

TERRY   It's nothing, Mum. Nothing.

TOM   She wants to know, so tell her.

TERRY   I can't. Not now. Not straight after being offered a house.

TOM   That's bait, you dunderheaded nit!

MUM   Is there something I should know then, Terry?

TERRY   It's just that Karen and me, we was thinking.

KAREN   We'd done more than think, Terry. We'd arranged it.

MUM   (*to* TERRY) Arranged what, my precious?

TERRY   Mind, I suppose it could always be cancelled, couldn't it?

KAREN   (*grimly*) No, it couldn't, my precious.

TERRY   What I mean is, it's not definite. I mean, nothing's definite
in this world——

KAREN *(cutting in)* We're emigrating to Canada, Mum. *(She quickly backs towards the cocktail cabinet.)*

MUM *(triumphantly)* So I was right. *(Rising and going U.C.)* I knew there was something. The moment Terry went into his shell, I knew there was something. *(Turning.)* It's always been the same with Terry, Shirley. If he was ever a naughty boy, straight into his shell he'd go, and nothing would induce him to come out. Everything became muffled with him; and he went a bit deaf and started to stutter. And I couldn't be harsh with him, Shirley. I always forgave, even if he'd hurt me, gone against my wishes, got in with the wrong crowd: because he was never a leader, was my little boy. He was always led. *(Crossing to L. of sofa.)* Well, nothing changes, does it? Now he's being led across the ocean to Canada by that pregnant cow over there. When do you think you're leaving?

TERRY A week tomorrow.

MUM What, all of you?

KAREN No; Terry first. The rest of us will join him later.

MUM *(pacing the floor)* You'll never join him. You're going to desert him. Get him out of the way, and then find another fool of a man.

KAREN *(sitting next to TERRY and taking his hand)* He'd have to be a fool to take on five kids.

MUM Half a mo. *(To L. of sofa.)* I thought immigration people were supposed to be particular about who they let in, or didn't you tell 'em?

TERRY What?

MUM That you got a criminal record.

TERRY *(protesting)* I've got no such thing.

MUM What about the time the police got their mitts on you for assault?

TERRY I was innocent.

MUM Innocent? You gave yourself up.

TERRY I never. I only went to the station with an estimate and they fell on me about the other thing.

TOM *(grinning)* It could only have happened to you, mate.

KAREN The girl didn't pick Terry out at the identity parade, so don't start nothing.

MUM Then why did Terry say that within an hour of being got at he was starting to think he'd done it; and by five in the morning he was ready to confess?

TERRY Because they got me into a right state. Kept tripping me up, got me to say things I didn't mean.

MUM That can only happen when you got a troubled conscience. And you've still got it. Every time you see a copper you get the shakes. They never did find the bloke, did they?

KAREN (angrily) What you implying?

MUM Why, you got a troubled conscience too? (Crossing to U.C.) I'm not surprised. You perjured yourself, didn't you, Karen? Said Terry was with you, but they soon found out he wasn't. They'd have put the pair of you away, given half the chance. (Pacing the floor.)

TERRY (with feeling) You can say that again.

KAREN The police dropped their charges against us, so save your breath, Mum.

MUM (to TERRY after a moment's silence) Have you got a job to go to?

TERRY Yer.

MUM (turning) Doing what?

TERRY My trade, of course.

MUM Trade? You haven't got a trade.

TERRY I'm a chippy, aren't I?

MUM (looking at him in amazement) A chippy? You can't even hammer a nail in without being rushed to hospital with a broken thumb. Joints to you are something you buy at the butcher's. You try cutting a hole, and that's all you're left with : a bloody great hole. All you're good at is making shavings. I tell you, two weeks in Canada, and you'll be hanged for sabotage.

TOM Come off it. He's not as bad as all that.

MUM (to TOM) Of course he's not; if we're going to compare him with your electrical genius. Remember that house in Church Avenue? When the owner pressed the switch in his lounge, the lavatory light come on.

TOM (annoyed as he rises) Look, dear; if you're not satisfied, get yourself a new electrician.

MUM A little thing to remember, Shirley. Tommy don't like criti-

cism, can't stand being criticised. (*Crossing to chair* U.L.)
You must tell him he's brilliant all the time or he'll sulk
his way to the nearest prostitute. (*Sitting.*) Mind, I'm not
blaming either of you boys. It's the high pressure; this
constant worry of working against time. (*With a helpless
gesture.*) But then what's one to do? Lengthen the time,
build fewer houses? Would that be fair to the millions of
homeless? You see, Shirley, here we are doing a service
to the nation by giving people decent houses to live in——

TOM (*stirring it as he wanders* D.S.) Get out of it. Our houses
aren't decent, they're obscene. We must be the only
builders putting up condemned property.

MUM (*indignantly*) Pardon me, your dad never put up a jerry-
built house in his life.

TOM I'm not talking about Dad. I'm talking about how the
business started to go rotten when he snuffed it.

MUM So how do you account for the fact that profits have gone
up by two hundred and fifty per cent since the burial
service?

TOM Because you knocked up your prices, and got us to knock
up two houses in the time it used to take Dad to build
one.

MUM (*crossing to* TOM) Time and motion, dear. Time and motion.
And now perhaps you'll shut up, stop hogging the conversation. God, you're so simple at times. But I love him.
I love my little Tommy Tucker. It's the masochist in me.
He flays me alive, and I'm distracted with it. (*To* TERRY,
cheerfully as she sits on R. *arm of sofa.*) Now, why do you
want to go to Canada, son? Tell Mum. She'll understand.
And I'm sure she'll forgive and forget. She always has. She
always will.

TERRY Well, it's sort of wanting independence like, Mum.

MUM (*nodding understandingly*) Yes, well, of course you'll get
that in a strange country, with a wife, and six kids, and no
money. Yes, you'll be very independent. But go on, I'm
listening.

TERRY I'm fed up worrying myself sick about getting the work
done in time.

MUM So we'll take out the fine clause in the contract.

TERRY But it's more than that, Mum. It's being part of something that's all wrong. We're no better than con men.

MUM So. We'll build fewer houses, detached houses.

TOM Cor, that's asking for it, ain't it? What will keep them up? (*He turns to* SHIRLEY, *who smiles and takes his hand.*)

TERRY And there's this business of working a twelve-hour day, six days a week. It's a killer, Mum.

MUM So we'll make it a five-day week.

KAREN (*impatiently*) You've said all this before, Mum; but it never happens.

MUM (*kindly*) Why be so destructive all the time, Karen? Forget your sourness, your feeling of failure—be constructive for a change. (*Rising.*) If you like, Terry, you can have it in writing, and we'll get the House of Lords to witness it. (*To* KAREN.) Will that satisfy you? (*She glances at her watch and moves upstage.*)

KAREN (*her impatience making her angry as she rises and faces* MUM *U.C.*) It isn't just the work. It's you!

MUM Me?

KAREN You're inside him all the time scratching away at his ulcer.

MUM Ah, that's more like my daughter-in-law. That refined act was giving you cramp, wasn't it? But now you're back in your right position again : down on all fours, spitting away with your whiskers quivering.

KAREN Oh, no. You hope I'll forget what we're arguing about, go on to the mud-slinging. Well, I'm not. (*Crossing to L. of sofa.*) Terry needs order in his life. All you've ever given him is chaos. You say one thing, expect him to do something else. Having had to listen to you for so long, his mind's confused, it's punch-drunk with the battering it's had from you.

(*The phone rings.* MUM *stares at* KAREN *as she lifts up the receiver and speaks into it.*)

MUM Pilgrim 8822. Yes. (*Pause.*) Speaking. (*Her face freezes and she clutches the table for support.*) When? (*Barely audible.*) Are they hurt? (*Long pause.*) My God! My God! (*Replacing receiver.*) My God!

TOM What is it, Mum?

MUM   (*in a state of shock*) That was the hospital. Henry's been
       in a crash. His car overturned.
       (SHIRLEY *and* TERRY *rise.* KAREN *is transfixed.*)

TERRY (*slowly moving U.L. towards* MUM) What about the kids?

MUM   (*turning upstage*) He's being operated on.

TERRY (*hoarsely*) The kids, Mum. The kids.

MUM   He's afraid their condition's critical.
       (KAREN *sways, gives a little moan.* TERRY *springs to her
       assistance and they hold on to each other.*)

TOM   (*moving in a few paces as whimpering noises come from*
       KAREN) What happened, then?

MUM   (*completely numbed*) Didn't say.

TERRY We ought to get down there.

MUM   No point. He's phoning back to tell us about the kids.

TERRY (*comforting the weeping* KAREN) Might not be as bad as it
       sounds.

MUM   (*walking slowly down to sofa*) Let her cry, Terry. Let it
       come out. Best for it to come out.

KAREN (*through her tears*) I should have gone. If I'd taken them,
       it wouldn't have happened. Why didn't I go?

MUM   (*sitting*) It's unbelievable.

SHIRLEY It's the suddenness of it.

MUM   (*closing her eyes*) Poor little mites. What harm have they
       done? And there's my Henry—my first-born. Be merciful,
       God. Be merciful.

KAREN (*frantically as she attempts to get to the door*) Must go to
       the hospital. We should be at the hospital.

TERRY No, love, no.

KAREN (*struggling*) Must be near them.

TERRY We are near, love.

KAREN Might be something we could do.
       (SHIRLEY *crosses to where* TOM *is standing.*)

SHIRLEY (*quietly*) I feel an intruder, Tom. I don't think I ought to
       be here.
       (TOM *is too dazed to say anything.*)
       There's nothing I can do.

TOM   No.

SHIRLEY I mean, this is private grief.

TOM   (*nodding*) Yer.

(SHIRLEY *goes out.*)

KAREN (*as* TERRY *leads her to armchair* R. *where she sits*) Should have driven them home. It's all my fault. I should have driven them home.

TERRY (*glancing across at* MUM) You put the receiver on properly, Mum?

(MUM *stretches out an arm and feels the receiver.*)

MUM Yes, son.

(*Suddenly* SHIRLEY *is heard to scream and a moment or two later she flies into the room.*)

SHIRLEY (*shrieking*) He's upstairs!

TOM Who?

SHIRLEY Henry!

TERRY (*not comprehending*) Upstairs?

SHIRLEY In the guest-room!

TOM (*crossing below sofa and turning to stare at* MUM) Did you hear that, Mum?

MUM (*calmly as she takes a cigarette*) Well, he lives here, don't he?

TOM But you said he was being operated on.

MUM One of my little fibs, I'm afraid.

TOM Who was the phone call from, then?

MUM It was a wrong number.

(KAREN *and* TERRY *stare at* MUM.)

TERRY So it wasn't true about the accident?

MUM No, it wasn't.

TERRY (*almost out of his mind*) What made you say it, Mum?

MUM (*grimly*) I just wanted Karen to know a little of how I felt about losing my son. It was an eye for an eye, and I sincerely hope it made her think for once.

(KAREN, *her eyes blazing, lunges at* MUM *and* TERRY *has to use all his strength to drag her away.* TOM *quickly goes to his assistance.*)

KAREN You filthy stinking bastard! I'll kill you! I'll kill you!

TERRY Calm down, Karen. Calm down.

KAREN She had me dead with shock! And it was all lies!

(TOM *lights a cigarette for her.*)

MUM (*rising and crossing to* KAREN) No, it's not very nice to think you'll never see your children again. But you were

going to do it to me, Karen love, weren't you? You were
going to have Terry go off to Canada.

KAREN (*still in a state*) You really are a bitch, aren't you?

MUM (*turning back to the sofa*) She does get so emotional,
doesn't she?

TERRY You oughtn't to have done that, Mum.

MUM I'm sorry, son, but I don't agree with you. I'm a firm
believer in the freedom of the individual. And it's taught
Karen a salutary lesson. At least I hope it did, and there
won't be any more nonsense about disappearing to Canada.
Anyway, there can't be much feeling there, or she'd be
thrilled that there's nothing wrong with them. In fact,
if you ask me, I think she's rather sorry it's turned out——

KAREN (*with quiet intensity as she turns to the window*) Don't go
on, Mum. Don't go on. Or I shan't be responsible.
(MUM *stubs out her cigarette while* TERRY *sits in the armchair and rubs his stomach.*)

MUM (*brightly*) Cheer up, lads. The party will soon be starting.
(*Glancing at her watch.*) Gracious me, look at the time.
(*Almost gaily.*) All this sorting out of other people's wor-
ries has put me behind. (*She crosses to where* SHIRLEY *is
standing by the door. She notices* SHIRLEY's *goggle-eyed
expression.*) Something the matter, dear?

SHIRLEY It's Henry.

MUM What about Henry?

SHIRLEY He's in my room.

MUM So you said.

SHIRLEY But he's dressed himself up in my clothes!

MUM (*not at all disconcerted and with a kind smile*) You should
take that as a compliment, my dear. He only wears clothes
that are clean and pretty. Very particular is my Henry.
(MUM *goes out and* SHIRLEY *turns to gape at* TOM *as the*
CURTAIN *quickly falls.*)

ACT TWO

The same, three hours later.

When the curtain rises SHIRLEY *is sitting on the sofa. There are flowers in the vase on the table above the sofa. On the coffee table are a small evening bag and a saucer. A second saucer is on top of the cabinet and a third on top of the piano. Six champagne glasses line the top of the cocktail cabinet.*

SHIRLEY *glances round as* HENRY *enters with two more vases filled with flowers. Kicking the door shut, he gives* SHIRLEY *an embarrassed smile as he crosses to place a vase on top of the cabinet* D.R.

HENRY (*quietly, apologetically*) I won't be half a tick, and then I'll get out of your way.

SHIRLEY (*kindly*) Please don't go because of me.

HENRY (*surprised*) You sure?

SHIRLEY Of course I'm sure.

(HENRY *places the second vase on top of the piano.*)

HENRY I didn't think you'd want to be in the same room as me after what occurred.

SHIRLEY Well, we've all got our idiosyncrasies, haven't we? Is that the right word?

HENRY (*smiling as he crosses to* L. *of sofa*) It's a very nice word, Shirley. And it's very kind of you to think of it like that.

SHIRLEY I must have given you quite a turn coming in on you like I did.

(SHIRLEY *makes room for* HENRY *and he joins her on the sofa.*)

HENRY You're right there, Shirley. (*Sheepishly.*) Well, I mean, you can't help feeling a bit guilty being found with someone else's clothes on.

SHIRLEY I'm sure you can't. I apologise.

HENRY Good lord, it's not you who should be apologising, Shirley, it's me. Trouble is, if I get the urge I just can't stop my— my idiosyncrasy.

SHIRLEY (*understandingly*) Must be very difficult.

HENRY (*casually*) Those things I put on, would you let me wash them for you?

SHIRLEY Oh, I couldn't let you do that.

HENRY (*insistent*) But I'd like to.

SHIRLEY No, no. I wouldn't hear of it.

HENRY (*after a short silence*) You've got some lovely clothes, Shirley. You got good taste.

SHIRLEY Thank you.

HENRY I like your slip. Come from Marks and Spencer, didn't it? I got quite a few Marks and Spencer's.

SHIRLEY (*surprised*) You collect them, do you?

HENRY I've no other vices.

(KAREN *enters carrying a tin of nuts.*)

(*Politely, as he rises and crosses upstage.*) Can I help you, Karen?

KAREN (*crossing D.R. and filling the cabinet saucer with nuts*) You just go back under your stone.

(HENRY *wanders up to the piano.*)

SHIRLEY I wasn't really expecting to see you again tonight, Karen.

KAREN (*kneeling by the coffee table and filling the saucer with nuts*) I know, and that's what she was hoping for. With me out of the way, she'd have worked on Terry until she'd got him pleading for mercy and screaming not to be sent to Canada. (*Grimly.*) Well, I've waited too long. We're going. We're going.

SHIRLEY But I don't know why your husband didn't walk out and take you with him.

KAREN (*crossing to the piano*) Terry's got his reasons.

SHIRLEY I'm sure I wouldn't have gone to the restaurant, let alone come back here afterwards.

KAREN You're not used to her little ways.

SHIRLEY Why haven't you got out before now?

KAREN (*dropping the empty tin into the wastepaper basket*) Terry thought he ought to stay.

SHIRLEY Why?

KAREN (*not wanting to get involved*) He felt he owed it to Mum.

(She crosses to armchair R.)

SHIRLEY *(kneeling on the sofa)* Did she give you a tough time when you was courting?

(HENRY *helps himself to the nuts on the piano.*)

KAREN I summed her up after the first meeting. Mind, she wasn't so bad in them days, not quite so blatant about it. *(Sitting.)* Dad was still alive, you see, and he had a bit of a soft spot for me. In fact, it was him who quietly hinted to Terry to send out the wedding invitations after the ceremony. And that's what we did. She never spoke to me for the next six months. Best six months I've had with her.

SHIRLEY So she's always like this, is she?

KAREN Even Tom says that with her sons, she's almost human; but at the first sniff of perfume she takes to her broomstick.

SHIRLEY Then I've been let off rather lightly, haven't I?

KAREN Let off? She hasn't even started on you yet. She will. She'll find your weakness, and she'll drag it round the room in triumph. But I warn you. If you walk out of here tonight, you'll never come back. And if you stay it means bloody war.

HENRY *(taking the saucer with him as he moves D.C.)* I hope you do stay, Shirley.

KAREN *(glancing across at* HENRY*)* Have you apologised?

(HENRY *gestures for* KAREN *to shut up as he crosses* D.R.)

SHIRLEY Yes, he has.

KAREN Beats me why you don't control it, Henry.

HENRY I do try, Karen.

KAREN You can't, otherwise it wouldn't happen, would it?

SHIRLEY *(trying to be diplomatic)* He didn't harm no one.

KAREN Here, he hasn't been talking to you about it, has he? You haven't been going into details, Henry, surely?

HENRY *She* was very sympathetic, Karen.

KAREN Honestly, you're just an exhibitionist.

SHIRLEY Don't you think it sometimes helps if you talk it over with——

KAREN But he don't want no help, Shirley. He won't even go and see a psychiatrist. Will you?

HENRY No, not really.

KAREN You see. He wants to be a pervert.

SHIRLEY (*shocked*) That's not a very nice thing to say, Karen. He's not a pervert.

KAREN (*gazing thoughtfully at* HENRY) What is he then?

SHIRLEY (*after a moment's thought*) But I mean, he doesn't look like one, does he?

HENRY (*with a smile*) I must say I don't feel like one.
(TERRY *and* TOM *enter.* TERRY *crosses to the cocktail cabinet with a bottle of champagne and proceeds to fill the six glasses.* TOM *is smoking a cigar.*)

KAREN See? He even thinks it's amusing. (*As* HENRY *returns the saucer to the piano.*) Just why won't you go and see a psychiatrist?

TOM (*cheerfully*) Being got at, Henry?

KAREN I'm only trying to knock some sense into him. I mean, if he's allowed to go on like this, where will it end?

TOM With a warehouse full of washing.

HENRY (*embarrassed*) I'd rather we talked about something else if you don't mind.

TERRY Yes, leave him alone, Karen.

KAREN (*rising and going to join* TERRY) I tell you, Henry, if I'd found you wearing my clothes, I'd have throttled the life out of you.

TOM (*crossing to L. of sofa*) What's known I think in the trade as psychotherapy.

KAREN He wouldn't have done it again. Or anything else.

TOM (*sitting on L. arm of sofa and gesturing to* TERRY) He's the one I'd be laying into if I was you, Karen. I mean, he didn't exactly tear into Mum about the hospital business, did he?

TERRY Belt up, you.

TOM Well, did you?

SHIRLEY (*placing her feet on the floor*) I must say, I think I'd have expected a bit more from my husband.

KAREN (*moving in a few paces*) Stop poking your noses into something that's private. What Terry said or didn't say doesn't concern anyone but me and Terry. If I want to make something out of it, all well and good. But it's up to me. (*She shakes a friendly fist at* TERRY.)

TOM   Same could be said for Henry. What he does concerns only him.

HENRY   Leave me out of it, Tom.

TOM   But that's you all over, Karen. Every time Mum crucifies you, you resurrect yourself and make a beeline for Henry.

KAREN   You're dead cocky at the moment, aren't you, mate? Well, wait till she starts performing on you. You'll be shrieking for help.

TOM   And I'll get a lot from old ulcer chops, won't I? One thing for sure. He won't be going to Canada.

TERRY   I will.

TOM   You won't.

TERRY   I will!

TOM   You won't!

KAREN   (*crossing to L. of sofa*) Two can play at this prediction lark. You've given yours, I'll give mine now. You won't be marrying Shirley.

TOM   And who'll stop me?

KAREN   (*pointing to* SHIRLEY) She will. Shirley will.

SHIRLEY   (*quietly*) I've just realised what's wrong with this house. It needs a bit of love pumping into it, doesn't it?

TOM   You pump anything like that in here, and it would just run down the walls like condensation.

KAREN   And Mum would go round soaking it up for herself.

TOM   (*wandering U.L.*) No, what I'd do is bring in the heavy lead ball; let it go crashing against the walls.

KAREN   (*grinning*) And where's Mum, Tom? Where is Mum?

TOM   (*grinning as he crosses to R. of* KAREN) Inside the house, Karen. Right bang in the way of the ball of lead. (*Slamming fist into palm.*) BIFF! Straight on her napper. And her brains go dancing down the stairs.
(TOM *and* KAREN *chuckle.*)

SHIRLEY   (*kneeling again on the sofa*) It's winning, isn't it? The atmosphere's winning. You're breathing it in, and it's winning.

TOM   (*crossing to her*) Only while we're in the house, Shirley. Once out of here and the air gets to it, cleans it away.
(KAREN *sits in armchair* R. *while* TOM *wanders below sofa and* U.L.)

TERRY I can understand Karen feeling the way she does. But you've got no excuse. For all his faults Henry at least appreciates everything Mum has done for him. But not you. Never you.

(MUM *quickly enters, wearing a cocktail dress.*)

MUM (*to* HENRY) Here, do me up at the back, will you? It's come undone again.

(HENRY *fastens the top hook of the dress.* MUM *gives* SHIRLEY *a dark look and* SHIRLEY *removes her feet from the sofa.*)

(*Smiling.*) Isn't it a lovely dress, Shirley?

SHIRLEY (*crossing D.R.*) Yes, lovely.

MUM Yes, I thought you've been looking a bit green round the gills lately. We'll light the bonfire and set off the fireworks after we've done our party pieces. Don't little boys love fireworks, Shirley? Especially bangers; and I've got them a lot of bangers.

HENRY (*stepping back*) How's that, Mum?

(MUM *feels the dress and sees if the arms fit.*)

MUM (*amazed*) Brilliant, quite brilliant. You've done a magnificent job, Henry. Fits skin tight now it does, and yet I've got all the movement I need. (*Turning.*) What a tragedy for us women you didn't take up dress-designing. With those dexterous fingers and that imagination, you'd have conquered Paris.

HENRY (*embarrassed*) It was only the top hook that needed fastening, Mum.

MUM It's his modesty that's so humbling, I find. If he climbed Everest it would be the same. It was only twenty-nine thousand feet that needed climbing. No wonder you can bring on my tears, son.

(*The doorbell rings.*)

(*Flicking her fingers.*) Answer it, Henry. (*Gliding D.S. as* HENRY *goes out.*) Hand round the champagne, Tommy. It's time to drink the loyal toast.

(TOM *crosses to the cocktail cabinet and takes a glass to* KAREN.)

Forty years ago, the beginning of a wonderful marriage— two people becoming one. (*Gazing at* SHIRLEY *who moves along to make room for* MUM.) I was a bit like you, Shirley, at the time. (*Sitting.*) Wanting to disappear through the plaster when somebody looked at me—fumbling for words—not really pretty, either. But I did have one magical quality, and this is where we differ, Shirley. I had a delicious sense of humour, which I've still got, of course.

TOM (*grinning as he hands a glass of champagne to* MUM) And you can't suppress it, can you, Mum?

MUM (*chuckling as she takes the glass*) No, I can't.

TOM (*handing* SHIRLEY *the second glass*) It keeps wafting over us all like poison gas.

(TOM *bends over the sofa and* MUM *holds his head down.*)

MUM (*merrily*) And he takes after me, Shirley. He's got the same sense of fun. No wonder we're inseparable, Tommy. It's frightening really. I believe one can be jailed for it.

SHIRLEY For what?

MUM Incest, Shirley. Incest.

(SHIRLEY *quickly rises and backs away as* TOM *frees himself.*)

(*To* TOM.) Would you go to jail for me, son?

TOM I'd see a bus run over you first. (*He crosses to the cocktail cabinet.*)

MUM (*with renewed chuckling*) All these quips of his. I suppose I should write them down, let posterity have a good chuckle.

(TERRY *wanders* D.R. *with his glass as a worried-looking* HENRY *enters.*)

HENRY It's plot twelve at the door, Mum.

(TOM *hands him a glass and then returns to the cocktail cabinet.*)

MUM (*surprised*) What's he want?

HENRY He's a bit annoyed, Mum. He and his wife moved in a couple of hours ago, after coming all the way from Edinburgh, only to find the floorboards weren't down in the kitchen.

MUM (*frowning*) So what's he expect us to do, then?

HENRY Go and put the floorboards down.

MUM (*staring at* HENRY) You're not serious?

HENRY I am. And he certainly is.

MUM   (*icily*) Tell him we've got a party on, but that I'll try and send someone round first thing in the morning.
(HENRY *goes out.*)
I ask you, what impertinence! Coming round here in the middle of the night, knocking us up, shouting the odds. They must think they bought us along with the house. (*Turning and looking across at* TERRY.) Still, it means you should do very well in Canada, Terry. That is if they don't have floorboards in Canada.

TERRY   I was about to put them down when I was called away on another job. Some idiot had fitted the wrong pipes to a gas-heater. When you turned on the jets, out spurted water.

MUM   That's no excuse, Terry.
(SHIRLEY *takes a sip of champagne.*)
(*Angrily to* SHIRLEY.) How dare you! Who the hell do you think you are?

SHIRLEY   (*bewildered*) Why, what have I done?

MUM   You took a sip of the champagne just then. I saw you.

SHIRLEY   Only because it was spilling over.

MUM   You haven't dropped any on my lovely carpet, have you?

SHIRLEY   No, it went on my dress.

MUM   That's all right, then. But nobody drinks until after the toast. My God, you must have been dragged up!

SHIRLEY   (*angrily*) Look, I'm getting fed up the way you're picking on me.

MUM   (*lightly*) Hello, hello, hello; another one with a persecution mania.
(*Broken glass is heard, and a furious Scotsman's voice shouts 'And you tell them that'.* TERRY *and* KAREN *quickly look out of the window* R. HENRY *enters dabbing his nose with a handkerchief. His tie and collar are ruffled.* MUM *moves to* L. *of* HENRY.) What's up, what's been going on out there?

HENRY   When I told him what you said, he got rather shirty.

TOM   (*grinning as he crosses to* R. *of* HENRY) Did he take a poke at you, Henry?

MUM   Did he, son?

HENRY   Yes, I'm afraid he did.

MUM Where is he now: flat on his back?

HENRY No, he's still standing in the porch; still wanting his floor-boards down.

(TOM *laughs as he goes into the hall.*)

MUM Get on the phone, Tommy. Nine-nine-nine, straight away. We'll have him for assault.

KAREN (*absolutely delighted as she joins* TOM) Won't be very good publicity, will it? No floorboards down in the kitchen.

MUM But heavens, they're not necessary at night. He's not sleeping in the kitchen, is he?

HENRY (*crossing to the mirror on top of the cabinet*) He and his wife want something to eat.

MUM (*returning to the sofa and sitting*) Well, there's a perfectly good café not half a mile down the road from where they are. People are getting to be so selfish.

(KAREN *and* TOM *re-enter.* TOM *takes up a position* R. *of piano while* KAREN *crosses to above armchair* R.)

HENRY Shall I invite him in?

(KAREN *and* TOM *laugh.*)

MUM You most certainly will not. I'm not having Fascists inside my house. You just go and slam the door in his face, son.

HENRY He's got it wedged with his shoe.

MUM Good. We'll have him for breaking and entering.

KAREN (*grinning as she crosses to* R. *of sofa*) You can't afford the publicity.

MUM (*her eyes narrowing*) Of course, you're enjoying this, aren't you?

KAREN (*nodding and laughing*) Yes. (*Crossing and sitting on piano stool.*)

TERRY (*moving in*) I'll go and fix the floorboards.

MUM No, you don't. Sit down.

TERRY But it won't take long.

MUM You're staying here. I've not finished with you yet.

(TERRY *sits in armchair* R.)

Henry, go and fix the floorboards. And at the end of it, I want every one of them creaking.

HENRY (*crossing upstage*) How will I do that?

TOM Just do the job as best you can, Henry.

(HENRY *goes out dabbing his nose.*)

MUM It's just not worth it. I've a good mind to chuck it. It's not
worth the worry. I have to carry everyone. Well, my poor
old bones are beginning to crack under the weight. No, I
think 'sell up' is the answer—retire—perhaps go to Canada.
(TERRY *makes an involuntary movement and spills some
drink.*)

TERRY (*rubbing the carpet with his handkerchief*) Sorry, Mum
Spilt some champagne.

MUM (*lightly*) Champagne's good for the carpet, Terry. It's like
a lover's kiss. Helps to bring out the bloom. (*Taking a sip
of her champagne.*) Did you know that, Shirley?
(SHIRLEY *doesn't reply as she sits* D.L.)
(*Gazing at* SHIRLEY *with interest.*) Don't you ever speak,
dear? Tell me, what do you do for a living? Clean out the
mortuary: something like that, is it?

TOM Just how long we supposed to hold this glass in our hand?

MUM (*rising and going to refill her glass*) Yes, it's high time we
remembered Dad. Forget meanness, pettiness, greed. Think
of goodness, kindness, love.
(TERRY, KAREN *and* SHIRLEY *rise as* MUM *crosses to* C.)
And we can do that by thinking of my husband, your
father, for a few quiet moments. Dad always saw good
in people, always wanted to help. He gave me everything
I ever wanted; and his last sweet words to me were—and
there were tears in his eyes when he said it—'I did try,
Mum. I did try.'

TOM (*his expression one of amused incredulity*) He never!
(KAREN *and* TERRY *sit.*)

MUM (*frowning*) What you mean he never?

TOM I was there, remember? I heard what he said.

MUM He said what I've just said.

TOM He never! He looked slowly up at the ceiling, sighed, and
said very hoarsely, but very clearly: 'Now perhaps I'll
get a bit of bloody peace!'

MUM (*dangerously quiet as she gazes at* TOM) Excuse me, pet;
that come after. And what he said was: 'It's been peace,
perfect peace.'

TOM Why should he have said that?

MUM Because that's how he felt.

TOM He didn't have no feelings left. For forty years you'd gone round gobbling them up.

MUM (*snapping out the words*) I couldn't have, or he wouldn't have given me so much joy! (*As* TERRY *places his glass on the cocktail cabinet.*) Where do you think you're going?

TERRY I'm off into the kitchen if you two are starting.

MUM You sit down.

TERRY But, Mum, every year it's the same old stuff that's trotted out——

MUM This is my day, and I'll spend it the way I choose.
(TERRY *sits in armchair* R. *and* MUM *turns to* TOM.)
Won't I, love?

TOM (*crossing to* L. *of sofa*) I'm not your love.

MUM You are. You belong to me, and I'm having you. If I could I'd stuff you, put you in one of those cabinets over there along with my other beautiful possessions. And that's love for you. No wonder they're devoted to me, Shirley.

TOM (*almost speechless*) Devoted? Devoted? None of us can wait to get clear of you. In fact, Henry's already gone. He went the quick way : round the bend. Terry there, he's off to Canada.

MUM (*quickly*) He's not going.

KAREN (*rising*) He is.

MUM (*plaintively as she crosses to* TERRY) He said he wouldn't. You promised faithfully you wouldn't.

TERRY When did I do that, Mum?

KAREN (*impatiently as she takes up a position* R. *of* TERRY) You didn't, Terry. Take no notice of her.

MUM (*grinning*) But you're going to take notice, aren't you, Terry?

TERRY (*firmly as he glances up at* KAREN) I don't think so, Mum.

MUM (*bending over the chair and speaking softly*) I think so, Terry; because we've got a secret, haven't we? And we wouldn't want it to come out, would we? Not in front of Karen. She'd never trust you again.
(KAREN *quietly crosses to the glass cabinet.*)

TERRY Leave it alone, Mum.

MUM (*crossing to sofa*) Only if you say you're not going to Canada.

TERRY (*rising*) Look, stop getting at me. I'm always on your side, always giving you the benefit of the doubt, sticking up for you, so leave it alone.

MUM What do you do with the money then, Terry?

TERRY Shut up, Mum.

MUM (*sitting*) The five thousand quid. Every time a thousand quid. What do you do with it, Terry?

TERRY (*crossing to* KAREN) Get your coat, Karen. I'll see you outside.

MUM A thousand smackeroos in fivers when you tell me Karen's pregnant. What have you bought Karen with it?

TERRY (*uncomfortably as he wanders up to the window*) You swore you'd never let on, Mum.

TOM (*gaping as he crosses to* R.C.) She gives you a thousand quid each time Karen's expecting?

MUM (*in a chatty mood*) I only make one proviso, dear. Terry's got to be the father. Well, as I always say, Shirley, better to nip these things in the bud. I mean, now that she knows, we don't want her turning herself into a public company.

TOM (*to* TERRY) You've kept this quiet, haven't you?

SHIRLEY (*to* MUM) But why? Why?

MUM I'd have thought it was obvious. (*She pats the sofa and* SHIRLEY *sits.*) By the time the second baby's bumping around inside Mummy, Daddy's become a nanny because Mummy can't bend, Mummy gets tired, Mummy don't want to know. Well, Daddy's not made that way. He needs the attention, 'cos Daddy's the biggest baby of the lot. So what does he do? He gets all frustrated and sour, and looks around for another breast to feed off. And that's precisely why I've been giving Terry the money. To save the marriage, give him an outlet other than women. Let him get his excitement from the dogs or the casino.

TOM (*almost jeering*) You might as well try persuading a starving lion to pick your teeth for you as expect us to believe that load of codswallop. You gave him the thousand quid hoping he'd blew it on some bird, and so get Karen hotfooting it to the nearest divorce court. A thousand quid a go!

TERRY (*with a wary eye on* KAREN *as he moves towards her*) It

was only two hundred and fifty to start with. The first
thousand come when I told her Karen was pregnant again.
And she said she'd give me a thousand quid every time a
baby was on its way, provided I spent the money on myself, and didn't let on about it.

KAREN *(gleefully as she turns and takes a few paces into the room)*
And I'll tell you why.

TERRY *(frowning)* No, you won't, Karen.

KAREN *(fervently)* Sorry, love, I can't miss the opportunity. It'll
never come again.

TERRY But it's not true.

(KAREN crosses up to TOM while TERRY sits D.R.)

KAREN Of course it's true; and it didn't take me long to twig it
neither. Terry still won't hear of it. This is why: as soon
as my mum heard about the second being on the way, she
started on at me about not allowing a decent interval in
between. Started going on about my heart; not being good
for my heart.

TOM *(surprised)* Why, you got a dicky heart, then?

KAREN No. Besides, kids come out of me like a bullet. *(Sitting in
armchair R.)* But you know what mothers are. I was supposed to have had pleurisy when I was a kid, and ever
since then she's maintained I'm delicate. Me, delicate!
Said the illness must have affected my heart. All fantasy,
but with my mum fantasy's another word for fact. And
she told me she'd had a quiet word with Terry's mum
about my poor heart, and Terry's mum had agreed it
wasn't right for me to have another baby so soon.

*(MUM frowns as KAREN crosses to the sofa. KAREN starts to
laugh.)*

And so what did Terry's mum do about it? She gave Terry
a thousand quid and said, 'How quickly can you get the
next brat under way?'

TERRY She never, Karen. She never said that.

KAREN *(touching the side of her temple as she goes upstage)* It's
what was going on back here, don't you worry. *(Still
laughing.)* For years she's been waiting for me to drop
down dead.

(SHIRLEY quickly moves away from MUM and sits D.L.)

She thought she was going to commit the perfect murder. And all she's been doing is paying us for having kids that we wanted anyway.

TOM (*grinning admiringly*) And where's the money now?

KAREN (*almost weak with laughter*) I've got it stowed away, little Tommy Tucker. Canada, here we come!
(*She stretches out her arms and she and a delighted* TOM *swing each other round.*)

TERRY (*quickly to* MUM, *from whom he receives a withering look*) I had to tell her about the money, Mum.

TOM This is fantastic, Karen! Fantastic!

TERRY I mean, you try hiding a wad of fivers from a wife, Mum. It's not easy.
(TOM *can hardly contain himself as he addresses* MUM *from above the sofa.*)

TOM You boobed bringing this one into the open, didn't you, darling?

KAREN (*wiping the tears of laughter from her eyes*) But you haven't heard the last of it yet, Tommy. She gave Terry a thousand quid because of the latest one that's on the way. Only there isn't one!

TERRY (*surprised*) There isn't one?

KAREN No, I'm not pregnant, Terry.
(KAREN *falls into armchair R.*)

TOM (*falling about with laughter*) You've done it, Karen! You've out-mummed Mum!

TERRY (*crossing to* MUM) I thought she was, Mum. It's what she told me.

TOM (*pointing to* MUM) Look at her! Just look at her! She can't speak! You've clobbered her into silence!
(TOM *sits on the sofa. Gradually the laughter fades and everyone's eyes turn on* MUM, *who is gazing thoughtfully out front. Silence.*)

MUM I don't want to do it, children, but I don't see no way out.

TOM Do what?

MUM Hand Henry over to the police.

TERRY (*startled*) Hand Henry over to the police?

MUM I can't possibly cope with him on my own. He'll just have to go inside while I work things out.

TERRY But you can't do that to him, Mum.

MUM (*regretfully*) He's got to be made to see it's wrong, son. Besides, he's getting worse. I mean, I can't get into his room now for lingerie. He's got to be watched morning, noon and night, and with you gone, I just won't have the time.

TOM So let him go for treatment somewhere.

MUM They'll give him treatment in prison, and it'll give me a chance to wind up the business. I'm sorry, but I just don't see no alternative.

KAREN (*grimly*) Unless Terry stays.

MUM (*nodding*) As you say, Karen love, unless Terry stays.

TERRY But that's blackmail.

KAREN She'd never do it.

MUM Want to bet?

TOM She'll do it all right.

MUM (*rising*) I'm only doing it on humanitarian grounds. My eldest needs help. Well, now, what kind of a Mum would I be if I didn't see he got that help?

TOM Yes, that's just about the kind of help you would give; sling someone in the nick for six months.

MUM I'm not slinging him in the nick. Terry is. If he was really concerned about Henry he wouldn't be leaving.

KAREN (*shifting her position*) I agree with Mum. Henry should be locked up. That way he might come to his senses, might even make a man of him.

MUM (*crossing to refill her glass*) That's only because you don't want Terry to stay. You're not saying it on humanitarian grounds.

KAREN I'm saying it because I think it'll do Henry good.

MUM (*coming down to R. of armchair*) How will it? How can six months in jail do him any good?

KAREN Look, you're the one who's going to put him there.

MUM (*crossing to C.*) On humanitarian grounds, Karen. Not hypocritical grounds.

KAREN Whatever the reason, he's going, isn't he?

MUM That depends on Terry.

KAREN Then he's going.

MUM (*gently to* TERRY) Is that right, son?

(TERRY *quickly moves away and sits* D.R.)
Would you turn your back on your big brother? Would you let him go to jail without trying to do something about it?

KAREN (*exasperated*) It's not up to Terry. You're the one that's going to tell the police.

MUM (*crossing to* TERRY) Only because I won't be able.to cope without Terry. (*In her sing-song voice of remembrance.*) Well, son; what's it to be? He's the one who dragged you out of the pond when you was four years old. Remember? He was the one who let you play with his clockwork train that puffed smoke. Chug, chug, chug, chug; wheee-ee! Remember? He was the one who went out early one morning and come back with seventy-two conkers, which he gave all to you, remember?

TOM (*impersonating* MUM's *voice as he rises and crosses to* C.) He was the one who took away your chair that time and you had a dislocated bum for six weeks. Remember?

MUM (*furiously*) He never did.

TERRY He's never done anything rotten to me in his life.

TOM I know he hasn't. It's just that I find Mum's sentimental goo nauseating.

MUM (*factually to* TERRY) Very well. He was the one who waited all night for you while the police tried to pin that assault charge on you. He was the one who comforted you when you came out a nervous wreck. Remember?

TERRY All right, I don't want Henry to land up in the nick.

KAREN But it's for his own good, Terry. It's humanitarian.

MUM (*returning to the sofa*) My God, she's quick! You've got to admit she's quick, Shirley. Notice how she's pinched my argument. Well, it won't wash, dear. If you want to be humanitarian as you call it, you'll see he don't go to jail.

SHIRLEY (*placing her glass on the coffee table and then sitting again* D.L.) I don't think he should go to jail either.

MUM (*glancing quickly round at* SHIRLEY) I do wish you'd keep that mouth of yours—— (*Suddenly realising what* SHIRLEY *has said, and mollifying her tone.*) You don't, dear? (*She sits.*)

SHIRLEY No, I don't.

MUM   (*knowledgeably to* KAREN) This one's taken O level. (*To*
SHIRLEY.) You've taken O level, haven't you?

SHIRLEY   No, I went to a secondary modern.

MUM   Ah, like me, a late developer. But don't worry about it;
you've got it, dear, you've got it. (*To* KAREN.) Yes, we've
got an educated woman here, Karen; and she says Henry
shouldn't go to prison. Well, I mean, you can't argue with
an educated woman, can you? Be fair, now, Karen. You
can't, can you?

SHIRLEY   He'd only be ridiculed in prison, wouldn't he? And nobody
wants him to be ridiculed, surely?

MUM   Let's ask them, dear. (*To* TERRY.) Do you want him to be
ridiculed, Terry?

SHIRLEY   It wouldn't help his illness. Make it worse.

MUM   Much worse.

SHIRLEY   He'd only come out, do it again, be given a longer sen-
tence.

MUM   Until one day, he'd go in and never come out. Just because
of your selfishness, Terry.

SHIRLEY   Oh, I disagree with you there, I think Terry should go to
Canada.

MUM   (*turning to gaze at* SHIRLEY) You do?

SHIRLEY   Yes, definitely.

MUM   You're a bit of a cretin on the quiet, aren't you?

KAREN   I thought she was an educated woman?

MUM   Yes, she certainly fooled me, did you? (*Rising and
crossing to* SHIRLEY.) God, you're so facile, Shirley. Everything on the surface, but take a closer look and what do
we find? You've got false eyelashes. She's got false eyelashes. And one's come unstuck.
(MUM *laughs with sadistic pleasure as* SHIRLEY *puts a hand
to her eye.* TERRY *rises and goes upstage.*)
(*Suddenly taking the hand and looking at it.*) And false
nails. She must bite her nails. (*As* SHIRLEY *wrenches her
hand away.*) What a nervy little duckling you are. (*With
a glint in her eye.*) What else is false about you, dear?
What else are you trying to hide? You're not wearing a
wig, are you? Let's see if you're wearing a wig.
(SHIRLEY *immediately puts her hands over her ears.*)

SHIRLEY (*angrily as* MUM *tugs at her hair*) Let go of my hair!

MUM What are you hiding your ears for? Let's see your ears.

SHIRLEY No!

MUM Why not?

SHIRLEY They're ugly! Ugly!

MUM (*grinning away*) Let's see, then! (*Wrenching away* SHIR-LEY's *hand and looking.*) My God, you're right, aren't you? (*Glancing round at* KAREN.) Have you ever seen ears like that before? (*Looking again.*) They're enormous! Must take you about a week to wash 'em. Here, come and have a look at these ears. She's got bruiser's ears! And they're all mottled. (*As* SHIRLEY *manages to free her hand and go to* TOM.) God, I don't think I've ever seen such an ugly sight. They quite turned my stomach over.

SHIRLEY (*gritting her teeth*) Shut her up, Tom, please!

MUM (*sitting on sofa*) Why, are you ashamed of them?

SHIRLEY Yes, I am.

MUM So you should be.

SHIRLEY I think they're horrible.

MUM (*changing her position*) They're revolting.

SHIRLEY (*intently as she crosses to below piano*) All right, revolting. I agree with you.

KAREN Wave good-bye, Tom. She's found her weak spot.

TOM Not this time. I'm marrying her, Mum.

MUM But have you seen her ears?

TOM There's nothing wrong with her ears.

MUM They're repulsive. (*To* SHIRLEY.) Aren't they repulsive?

SHIRLEY Yes!

MUM You see, she keeps agreeing with me.

TOM (*crossing to* SHIRLEY) Because she's got a thing about them.

MUM Well, I'm sorry, but I've got an aversion to anything repulsive. I can't help it, it's part of my nature. Makes me cringe, Shirley, makes me creep all over, I feel affronted. You'll have to leave.

TOM If she leaves, I leave.

MUM What, with those ears? You could live with those ears?

TERRY (*crossing to* C.) Pack it in, Mum. She can't help it, can she?

TOM (*angrily*) But there's nothing wrong with her ears!

KAREN Shirley thinks there is, and that's what Terry's getting at.

TERRY (*to R. of sofa*) It's too easy to knock at something that people are sensitive about, no matter how stupid it might be.

MUM That was very poignantly said, Terry. Very poignantly said. You should have been a poet, darling.

(TERRY *moves away* R.)

(*Gazing at* SHIRLEY *with interest and speaking conversationally.*) Tell me, dear, do they let in much of a draught?

TOM (*grimly*) You'd like Shirley and me to clear off now, is that it, Mum?

MUM (*gaily, as she picks up her champagne and rises*) I'd like to get on with the party, my precious, when you've done with your moaning and groaning.

(MUM *walks upstage.* KAREN *rises.* TERRY *collects his glass from the cocktail cabinet and joins* KAREN. SHIRLEY *comes down to L. of sofa.* TOM *takes up a position above the sofa.*)

Don't forget, this is supposed to be my day. (*In her sing-song voice of remembrance.*) When I have all my little children round me, and we remember with respect our dear old dad who was lovely. (*Turning.*) I expect he's listening in. (*Looking up.*) Are you watching us, Dad? Are you here? If you're here, give us a sign.

KAREN Careful, we might have the house down on top of us.

TOM That could be just normal routine with our houses. No, do something useful, Dad: get the guvnor to turn her into a pillar of salt.

MUM (*ignoring* TOM) I bet he's smiling—thinking to himself: 'They haven't changed, have they? There's Mum standing out from all that deceit like a twinkling halo; yet still loving, always loving. Ah! And who is that new face I see? It must be a girl friend of Tommy's. Strange what men find attractive. Like clodhopper's ears.'

(KAREN *sits in armchair* R. *and* TERRY *sits on the left arm.* SHIRLEY *sits* D.L.)

TOM (*warningly*) You're at it again, Mum. One more word and I'll——

MUM (*remonstrating*) It's not me, it's Dad. I'm just telling you what he's saying. Blimey, isn't he even allowed to give an opinion now?

TOM He's dead!

MUM He's still got a right to be heard! (*Gesturing for everyone to rise.*) And now for the toast, children.

KAREN (*crossing D.R.*) About time.

(SHIRLEY *picks up her glass.*)

MUM I heard that, you drunken hag. Is that what you've been waiting for? You haven't got D.T.s, have you?

TERRY (*with bored exasperation as he joins* KAREN) Mum!

MUM It's just that I've noticed her twitching.

TOM Give us the toast before my arm drops off!

MUM (*moving downstage and gazing out front*) Well, here we are, Dad. All together as a family, paying our respects to you. Same last year, be the same next year. You are our father in this faithless world. You are the rock upon which we stand. We are united here in front of you, Dad; and once a member, always a member. No one will ever leave, because if he does, he will destroy me and you. And they are our children, and have not it in their hearts to destroy their mum and dad: because it is us, you and me, Dad, who will be mortally wounded; and the pain, the awful pain, will be such as no man has ever borne before.

(*During this speech* TOM *glances at his watch and* KAREN *mutters under her breath.*)

KAREN That's it.

(*An angry* KAREN *turns to go out but is restrained by* TERRY.)

MUM And our children won't want that, I'm sure. So toss us some of that love of yours, Dad.

KAREN (*returning to D.R.*) That'll be nice.

MUM (*with an edge to her voice*) That we may forgive those who live by trying to drive a wedge between us all. And turn their eyes, so that they may see the error of their ways. Well, here you are, Dad. I'll be joining you soon.

TOM I bet that give him a fright.

MUM So be patient, Dad. Be patient. (*Raising her glass and with her back to the audience.*) To Dad.

KAREN
TOM   {(together) Dad.
TERRY

(MUM *drains her glass and promptly sings 'O God our Help in Ages Past' in a raucous voice. Not knowing the rest of the verse, she substitutes 'Tee Tah' for the words.*)

MUM That was his favourite hymn, Shirley. His favourite hymn. (*Crossing to the sofa and sitting.*) Well, now, I've done my solo bit. It's your turn now, Terry.
(KAREN *sits in armchair R. while* TOM *sits D.L. and* SHIRLEY *sits on the arm.* TERRY *crosses to the piano and plays the first short tune he ever learned, before crossing to sit on the arm of* KAREN's *chair.*)

MUM (*with motherly pride as she looks at* SHIRLEY) You weren't expecting that, were you? That's why I keep the piano: in the hope he'll take it up again. If only he'd persevered, he'd have been resident pianist at the Festival Hall by now. (*Glancing at* TERRY.) You really ought to take it up again, Terry. You owe it to culture.

TERRY You've got a short memory, Mum. After five lessons, the instructor paid me not to come back.

MUM (*to* SHIRLEY) Five lessons; that's all he had. And yet he's able to produce that magic sound. Another five, and he'd have played a concerto. I think what it was, Shirley, he was frightened of the talent he knew was inside him. (*Brightly to* TOMMY.) And what are you going to do for us, little Tommy Tucker?

TOM (*crossing to C.*) I'm going to recite a poem.

MUM (*roguishly*) Yer, well, I bet we won't find this one in the Golden Treasury. Let's be having it.

TOM There was a young lady of Bow,
Who had it off with ten men in a row;
Because as she said,
When I get into bed,
I forget what the word is for no.
(MUM *shrieks with laughter.*)

MUM Oh, very good; very ribald.

KAREN (*grinning as she rises*) I think I can do better than that, Tom.

MUM   (*frowning*) Here, I don't want no filth in this house. This is a spiritual moment for me.

KAREN   Very well, I'll sing Ave Maria.

MUM   No, you won't, mate! (*To* SHIRLEY.) She's tone deaf, you know.

KAREN   I'm nothing of the kind.

MUM   And what's worse, she don't realise it. So the suffering is all one-sided. Hearing her sing is like having an abscess under a wisdom. Besides, I want to hear our little friend here do something.

(KAREN *sits again*.)

(*To* SHIRLEY.) It's your turn now to entertain us, dear.

SHIRLEY   (*with quiet intensity as she shakes her head*) No.

MUM   Yes.

SHIRLEY   No.

MUM   I said yes.

SHIRLEY   I'd feel a fool.

MUM   (*with an edge*) This is my day, Shirley, and I want you to entertain me.

SHIRLEY   I'd be too embarrassed.

MUM   (*angrily*) Will you stop thinking of yourself all the time, and get up and do something.

SHIRLEY   (*as* TERRY *rises—fiercely*) So that you can have a cheap laugh? No!

MUM   Yes!

SHIRLEY   You can't make me, you bully! You can't make me do a thing.

MUM   (*pointing to* TOM) I can stop you marrying him.

SHIRLEY   (*rising and crossing to* R. *of* MUM) No, you can't; because the more you try, the harder you'll find it! And I shan't be like Karen neither. Brainwashed so that I get to the stage when I can look on attempted murder as a bit of a giggle! Because once the reception's over, I shan't be coming here again. I'm not having you staring at me and talking about me as if I'm some sort of an experiment of yours. (*Sitting on* L. *arm of sofa*.) No, your days of pomp and circumstance where I'm concerned are numbered, because you've got nothing I want that I can't take for myself. I don't need anything from you!

MUM   (*spitting out the words*) You'll need a sedative when I tell.
you Tommy's already married!
(*A startled* SHIRLEY *rises and looks at* TOM.)

TOM   (*shaking his head*) It's not true, Shirley.

MUM   (*conversationally*) Still, it's shut her up—given us a bit of
respite. God, fancy having to put up with that voice
twenty-four hours of the day. It's so shrill, so penetrating.
(*Rising and going to* L. *of sofa.*) And, remember, I only
seem to bring out the best in people, so God help you, son.
Personally I preferred last year's exhibit. What was her
name?

KAREN   (*involuntarily*) Heather.

SHIRLEY   (*staring at* TOM) So there was a girl here last year.

TOM   Yes, yes, there was, Shirley.

MUM   (*wandering to above sofa*) You thought you was the first,
didn't you? I've congratulated two like you; and always
on this day.

SHIRLEY   (*to* TOM) Is she lying again?

MUM   (*between* SHIRLEY *and* TOM) I wonder who it'll be next
year?

SHIRLEY   (*still staring at* TOM) You've been engaged twice before?

TOM   (*appealing to her*) The others must have done it for a laugh,
Shirley.
(SHIRLEY *moves away* L.)

MUM   You was the one who split your sides.

TOM   There couldn't have been any real feeling there, Shirley,
because she was able to break them into little pieces.
She thinks she can do the same with anyone I bring
home.

SHIRLEY   Why didn't you tell me?

MUM   And spoil his fun?

TOM   I had to see if she could break you an' all.

MUM   (*crossing to* SHIRLEY) So there we are, dear. You're not the
first, are you?

SHIRLEY   (*intently, as she swings round on* MUM) No, I'm not. But
I'm going to be the last. There'll be no others after
me.

MUM   (*sneering*) You don't mind being used?

SHIRLEY   He can use me anyway he likes!

MUM   Even though he only got engaged to spit in my eye?

SHIRLEY   And I'm more than ready to spit in your other eye; the one that floats off on its own now and again!

(TERRY *and* KAREN *immediately exchange angry glances, while* MUM *gazes at* SHIRLEY.)

You've got a wonky eye that wanders, haven't you? It's wandering now.

TERRY   (*between gritted teeth as he crosses* D.R.) Shut her up, Tom!

(TOM *turns up to the cocktail cabinet.*)

SHIRLEY   After what she's put me through? She's got something wrong with her, so she gets her revenge by hunting out other people's weaknesses.

(*Silence.*)

(*Not comprehending.*) What's the matter; don't you see? This is where you can get your own back on her. This is *her* weak spot.

(*Silence.*)

(*Bewildered.*) I'm only giving her what she gave me.

KAREN   (*quietly*) Stupid little bitch.

MUM   (*softly*) Yes, you shouldn't have brought that up, dear.

SHIRLEY   Why?

MUM   That eye that's giving you so much pleasure isn't wonky. There's nothing wrong with it. It's the other eye. The glass eye. The one that never moves.

SHIRLEY   (*horrified as she backs a few paces*) A glass eye?

MUM   If you've got a minute, I'll tell you the history of it. One hot day in August when Terry was a little boy, he crept into Henry's bedroom and took Henry's air-pistol. Terry was very excited about it. He ran up to me in the garden and pointed it in my face, and as he pressed the trigger with both hands he shouted, 'You're dead, Mummy.' And he laughed and laughed until he saw the blood spurting out. He had nightmares for about two years; and he's never looked me straight in the face since. (*Glancing across to* TERRY *as she moves downstage.*)

KAREN   (*rising*) He's paid for it.

MUM   So instead of being cruel to me, dear, you were being cruel to Terry. Reminding him of that hot day in August when he stung the life out of one eye. Didn't you, darling? But Mummy forgave, didn't she?

KAREN You've never forgiven.

MUM (crossing to TERRY) He's never forgiven himself. There's a difference.

(TERRY turns, smiles sheepishly and crosses to the sofa where he sits and nurses his stomach.)

KAREN But you won't let him forget, will you?

MUM I can't very well stop looking at him, Karen. It's him, the way he's made. Now, if Tommy had been the one who'd done it, he'd have looked up at me and said, 'What you want to get in the way for?' It wouldn't have been Tommy's fault.

KAREN (sitting on arm of sofa and putting an arm round TERRY) It was no one's fault. It was an accident.

MUM But Terry don't think so. And he never will. He deliberately blinded his mother in one eye. That's all he knows. (Sitting D.R.) And how's he going to repay her? By going to Canada and shooting out the other eye.

KAREN Why didn't you warn the little git about it, Tom?

SHIRLEY (bridling) I've done nothing I'm ashamed of. I'm not having her dictating to me.

KAREN Why, what's so special about you?

SHIRLEY (heatedly) I just wanted to ram it home to her that I'm no clay pigeon for her to shoot at whenever she gets the mood. (She crosses to TOM and marches him downstage.) And while we're about it, we might as well get some more details sorted out. (To MUM.) From now on I come first where Tom's concerned. He answers to me. I've already made up my mind where we're going to live, and it's not near here. And I know the kind of job Tom will soon be doing, and it won't be working for you. And I know just how many kids I'm going to have, and I tell you they won't be seeing nothing of Grannie One-Eye. Tom's mine, and I'm not having him cut in two. And I'm staying the weekend, 'cos I'm not going to be got rid of. So what do you say to that?

(TOM simply gapes at her.)

MUM (smiling sweetly) Nothing, love. Nothing.

SHIRLEY I've ripped out your tongue, have I?

MUM Beautifully.

SHIRLEY You've found somebody who can stand up to you, and you don't like it, do you?

MUM (*surveying* SHIRLEY *with the spyglass*) No, I love it. Do continue.
(SHIRLEY *finds* MUM'*s manner disconcerting, but puts a brave face on it.*)

SHIRLEY Yes, well, we're going for a nice walk now (*She crosses below the sofa to the french windows where she attempts to open the curtains. She then remembers the switch and presses it.*) and when I come back, I don't want to hear any more talk about the wedding, 'cos it's been settled. I've settled it. Me and Tom are getting married; and if you start up again, I'll break that monocle over your head. Come on, Tom.

MUM Go on, Tom.
(*There is a short silence while* MUM *grins at* TOM.)

TOM (*frowning*) Yer, well——
(MUM *continues to grin at* TOM.)

SHIRLEY Tom!
(TOM *shuffles awkwardly.*)
Tom!

TOM (*lamely*) Just you remember what she said, then.
(*After a moment's indecision,* TOM *starts to go out and* MUM *whistles as if calling a dog.* TOM *momentarily hesitates and then goes out. There is a short silence.*)

MUM Strange it should have had such an effect on her.

KAREN What?

MUM Mentioning her ears. They was quite nice ears really. A bit lumpy, but nothing to go berserk about.

KAREN You've lost him this time.

MUM Have I? (*She rises and crosses to R. of sofa where she looks down on* TERRY.) You can't get away from it, no matter how hard you try. Can you, Terry? That hot day in August.

KAREN (*shaking her head*) It's not on, Mum. It's not on. Is it, Terry? Tell her it's not on.
(*Silence.* MUM *gives a little chuckle as she crosses to the*

french windows and presses the switch. The curtains close.)
(*Urgently.*) You'll always have a conscience about her glass
eye, Terry. Whether you stay here and try not to look
at it, or go thousands of miles away and have it haunt
you. So it don't matter really, does it?

MUM   He'll never throw me and his brothers on the scrap-heap.

KAREN   Him out of the way won't affect the business.

MUM   Oh, yes, it will.

KAREN   (*rising*) But he's got no room for any more conscience.
Your glass eye takes up all the available space. (*To* TERRY.)
Doesn't it? Tell her we're going.

MUM   I can still see him bringing up that air pistol.

KAREN   Well, tell her, Terry. (*Going down on her knees.*) Look,
she's never going to love you like she loves the others; and
if you ask me you ought to be darn glad of it. Tell her
we're going. Please.

(HENRY *enters breathlessly through french windows.*)

HENRY   I've just had the most exciting night of my life!

MUM   Don't tell me. You broke into Dorothy Perkins in the High
Street.

HENRY   (*crossing to* R.C.) No, it's the police. They almost nabbed
me.

MUM   What, for laying floorboards?

HENRY   No, after that. I'd taken a garment—I suddenly got the
urge, you see—and I was just pinning a ten-bob note to
the clothes line when they leapt out at me. I managed to
lose them though; and they didn't get a proper look at
me. I've been running ever since. (*Sitting armchair* R.)

KAREN   (*going to above the sofa*) Well; I think it's a great pity
you wasn't caught, Henry. A scandal like this might have
helped to bring you to your senses.

TERRY   (*crossing to cocktail cabinet and pouring a brandy*) What
about the car?

HENRY   (*worried*) Oh, my God. I'd forgotten about the car. The
police are sure to find it because it's parked right outside
that house. And it's got a sari, a suspender belt and a
couple of pairs of panties in the front seat. All taken from
the same road.

(TERRY *hands* HENRY *the glass.*)

KAREN Good. Headlines across the front page of the local rag will serve you right, Henry. I'm sorry but I've got no sympathy for you at all.

HENRY Ah, but it wasn't my car, Karen.

TERRY Not your car?

HENRY No, I was still using yours.

KAREN (*aghast*) Terry's car!

TERRY (*shrieking as he crosses to* KAREN) But the police will think it's me!

(MUM *hoots with laughter as the* CURTAIN *falls.*)

ACT THREE

As the curtain rises TOM *is standing by the open french windows looking at the flickering bonfire.* SHIRLEY *is in the hall gazing upstairs.*

MUM (*off*) Put it on the bonfire, Henry!

HENRY (*entering with a drawer filled with underwear*) Couldn't you say it was yours?

MUM (*off*) I said put it on the bonfire.

(HENRY *goes into the garden.*)

SHIRLEY (*with a nervous giggle as she comes into the room*) It's a proper madhouse, ain't it?

TOM (*sulkily*) It's never anything else.

SHIRLEY Will the police come?

TOM Bound to. They'll trace the car to his house and then to here.

SHIRLEY Surely she won't let Terry take the blame?

TOM (*crossing to cocktail cabinet*) Give her half a chance she'd drive the black maria herself.

SHIRLEY But if Karen gets them to search Henry's room they'll know it was him.

TOM They'll have to hurry.

(MUM *enters carrying large cardboard box full of underwear, followed by* KAREN.)

KAREN But you can't let Terry take the blame!

MUM (*smiling brightly*) I keep telling you, Karen, it was his car.

KAREN (*almost screaming*) But it wasn't him who did the thieving! (*Both go out through french windows.*)

SHIRLEY (*crossing to the sofa*) It's a madhouse all right.
(*As* TOM *pours himself a glass of brandy.*)
I'll have one, too, if I may.
(*She sits.*)

TOM (*sitting armchair right*) Help yourself.

SHIRLEY What's wrong?

TOM Nothing's wrong.

SHIRLEY What is it, Tom?

TOM What's what?

SHIRLEY You've been off me since we went for the walk.

TOM Have I?

SHIRLEY You wouldn't take my arm. Never spoke. Why?

TOM No reason.

SHIRLEY Then come and give us a kiss.

TOM I'm too tired.

SHIRLEY (*crossing to* TOM) All right, I'll come and give you one.

TOM (*turning his head away*) Don't bother.

SHIRLEY (*angrily*) Look, am I being stood up or something?
(MUM *and* KAREN *enter from french windows.*)

MUM (*crossing to hall*) You see it from your husband's point of view, Karen, which is understandable. But I see it from the police's point of view simply because I'm a good citizen. (*Goes out.*)

KAREN (*quickly, to* SHIRLEY) Shirley, you'll tell the police it was Henry, won't you?

SHIRLEY I'd rather not give an opinion if you don't mind.

TERRY (*off*) But Mum!

KAREN It's not an opinion I want. It's the truth! (*Goes out.*)

SHIRLEY Because if I am being stood up you won't find it that easy. I'll have your Mum's bank account for breach of promise. (*Returning to sofa and sitting.*) I'm not like the rest you've brought here. When I'm hurt I get sore about it. And I've been hurt tonight.

TOM You know, I swear you're even beginning to look like my mum.

SHIRLEY Your mum? What a thing to say!

TOM (*rising*) It's been worrying me.

SHIRLEY Since when?

TOM Since you went for her.

SHIRLEY Well, it's what you wanted, didn't you? It's what you brought me here for; so's I'd fracture her all over.

TOM You took over.

SHIRLEY Took over?

TOM (*crossing above sofa*) Left me just standing. Didn't let me get a look in. Kept me right out.

SHIRLEY What are you talking about?

TOM (*to L. of sofa*) I should have been the one to beat Mum. Not you. You should have eased up, let me take over. But no, you had to hold on, streak past the winning post yourself.

SHIRLEY I just wanted to prove I loved you.

TOM That's the reply I'd have got from Mum.

SHIRLEY Will you stop comparing me to your mum!

TOM (*crossing to the piano*) I'd been so looking forward to grinding her into bits of dust, but you had to go and spoil it.

(MUM *enters with another cardboard box full of underclothes, followed by a panic-stricken* TERRY.)

TERRY But you can't send me to prison, Mum!

MUM (*cheerfully*) I don't think dishonesty should go unpunished, son.

TERRY But I've done nothing!

MUM I'd like to believe you, but it's the car, it gives you away. Even a mother can't be blind to that piece of evidence.

(*She and* TERRY *go out through the french windows.*)

TOM (*coming down to above sofa*) And not content with that, you had to get me jumping after you as if I was some sort of remote-controlled zombie.

SHIRLEY Who did?

TOM (*to L. of sofa*) You did. You ordered me to come for a walk with you, didn't you?

SHIRLEY I only thought it would be a good idea——

TOM You see. *You* thought. (*Wandering* D.L.) Always you; it's always you.

(KAREN *enters from the hall and crosses to* TOM.)

KAREN Tom, you won't let your brother go to jail.

TOM One of them's got to go.

(HENRY *appears from the french windows, sees* KAREN *and hurries out again pursued by* KAREN.)

And I was going to spill her all over the carpet tonight.

SHIRLEY (*sincerely*) I'm sorry.

TOM (*crossing to armchair R. and sitting*) It's done, ain't it? The damage has been done. It's got itself lodged in their memories now, and you can never dislodge memory. It's always there, to be brought out when it's mocking-hour for little Tommy Tucker.

(TERRY *enters from the french windows followed by* MUM.)

TERRY But Henry said he'd taken it. He admitted it all.

MUM (*passing* TERRY *and going into the hall*) Well, that's Henry, ain't it? Always after a little bit of limelight.

TERRY (*following* MUM) But I've been here all the time!.

MUM (*as she and* TERRY *climb the stairs*) Where's your proof, son?

TOM That's one thing the others have never tried to do: push me out of sight, and then get me to crawl out backwards.

SHIRLEY It's this house, Tom.

TOM It can't bring out what's not there, Shirley.

SHIRLEY Then I must have done it for love. (*Crossing to* TOM *and kneeling.*) Look, Tom, what if we got you back on top again? How would that be?

TOM Can't see how.

SHIRLEY Must be some way.

TOM I'd have to stay there.

SHIRLEY Oh, I'd see you did, Tom; I'd see you did. You could always side with Terry over this police business.

TOM No. We're on Mum's side over that.

SHIRLEY Are we?

TOM Yer. Just think of all the extra work for me if Terry goes off to Canada. (*He concentrates and then gives a little chuckle.*) I've got it, I can get back on top.

SHIRLEY (*eagerly*) How?

TOM By us two spending the night in Mum's bed.

(SHIRLEY'S *eagerness fades and there is silence.*)

SHIRLEY Spend the night in her bed?

TOM Yer. What do you say?

SHIRLEY I don't think I'd enjoy it, Tom.

TOM (*rising and crossing to above sofa*) You see, Mum was right. Just thinking of yourself all the time.

SHIRLEY But I'd be no good, Tom.

TOM (*turning*) That don't matter, Shirley. It's enough just to be lying there, hearing Mum thumping away on the locked door and screaming through the keyhole. She'd know only me could have thought of it, you see. I'd get the full credit, not you.

SHIRLEY But it don't seem right to me.

TOM (crossing to R. of sofa) Precisely, Shirley. Precisely. It can only work if it don't seem right. Believe me, the whole thing's got to be stinking rotten if it's going to have any effect on Mum.

SHIRLEY Can't we just pack our bags and go back to my place?

TOM (sitting) No, we can't.

SHIRLEY I know we couldn't have sex. I mean, my mum and dad, they're a bit old-fashioned; (Hopefully.) but there's always the park, dear.

TOM And what would the others think of me if I ran away now? I'd be finished in their eyes; a henpecked write-off. No, I can't leave; not until I'm back on top and Mum beaten. And I've got to be the one who beats her.

SHIRLEY (almost inaudibly) And if I won't?

TOM Well, that's 'that, ain't it? I mean, it shows we can't agree about nothing. No, this is a good test I've set you. If your love's worth more than a quick bunk-up behind the rhododendrons, you'll spend the night with me in Mum's room.

SHIRLEY Honest, Tom, you don't know what you're asking. I'd feel unclean.

TOM (rising and crossing to the french windows) You needn't; the sheets are changed once a week.

SHIRLEY That wasn't what I meant.

TOM (pointing a finger at her as he crosses above sofa towards SHIRLEY) You're off again, aren't you? Turning the conversation back on little Shirley. I'm not interested in what you mean. I'm not concerned. It's irrelevant. It's what I mean, what I feel, what I want. (Appealing to her.) In another instance, Shirley, it could be the other way round. But in this instance it's not. Everything has to be done with me in mind. Only in that way can I win, see? (Crossing to window R.) So make up your mind. What's it to be? (HENRY and KAREN enter through french window. TERRY enters U.S. and SHIRLEY sits D.R.)

KAREN (quickly) Henry, you can't let your brother take the blame for what you did.

HENRY (*wanting to be fair as he halts in front of the piano*) It's not as simple as that, Karen.

TERRY (*boggling*) It couldn't be more simple! You done it, and you're going to pay for it.

HENRY But, Terry, I get claustrophobia if I'm shut up anywhere.

TERRY You should have thought of that before you let yourself become perverted!

(MUM *enters U.S. and crosses to the coffee table where she takes a cigarette.*)

MUM You know, you surprise me, Terry. Trying to push it on to your brother, knowing what an adverse effect prison would have on him. That's the lot, son.

KAREN (*to* HENRY) She was the one earlier on who was all for letting the police know about your perversion.

(HENRY *crosses to armchair R. and sits.*)

MUM (*almost sadly*) God, some people: they'll stop at nothing, even try to set son against mother. (*She glances at her watch and goes towards the door.*)

TOM (*frowning as he bars her way*) Where you going?

MUM (*surprised as she holds out her cigarette*) Why?

TOM (*lighting* MUM's *cigarette*) I mean, you're not going to bed, are you? I mean, you'll have to be here for the police, won't you?

MUM (*staring at* TOM) I just want to see how the bonfire's going. (*And* MUM *jauntily goes out through the french windows.*)

TOM (*emitting a loud yawn*) I'm tired! (*Stretching his arms and crossing towards the door.*) Think I'll go to bed.

TERRY (*swinging* TOM *round*) You'll go nowhere till the police have come and you've told 'em it was Henry.

TOM Look, mate, we've all got our problems. Anyway, it's your first offence, ain't it?

TERRY It's not even my first offence!

TOM I was speaking legally, chum. Because if it's your first offence, you'll probably only be put on probation.

HENRY Terry.

TERRY (*crossing hopefully to* HENRY) Yes?

HENRY I'd be very grateful, if you'd ask for sixty-two other offences to be taken into consideration.

(TERRY *gives up and sits on the sofa.*)

KAREN (*trying to control herself as she moves downstage*) This is
how she always wins. Whenever there's a crisis, everyone
shoots off in a different direction. (*Crossing to* HENRY.)
Henry, if you was a man like Terry, you'd give yourself
up.

HENRY (*mildly*) Karen, if I was a man like Terry, none of this
would have happened.

KAREN So what are you then?

HENRY I'm only going by what you've always called me: a pervert.

KAREN Then here's your chance to reform.

HENRY But I like being one.

KAREN Oh, sorry, I didn't know. (*Crossing to the french windows.*)
Well, that's something to comfort you while you're sew-
ing your mail-bags, Terry.

HENRY As Tom said, Karen, it's only probation.

TERRY (*very much vexed*) Henry, I'm not having my mates thinking I go creeping off to get satisfaction from a clothes-line!
They'll start saying I can't be the father of my own kids.

HENRY (*sitting on R. arm of sofa*) Try to see it from my point of
view, Terry. This time I'd get probation. Next time, prison.
Whereas if I keep quiet, next time will be the first time,
so I'll just get probation. See, it gives me a bit of breathing space.

KAREN Wait! (*Sitting next to* TERRY.) The bloke who didn't have
no floorboards. He'd have seen Henry get in the car.

HENRY No, he'd already left, Karen.

KAREN Then he'd have seen it outside his house.

HENRY (*apologetically*) It's an unmade road, Karen; so I left the
car round the corner.

KAREN (*screaming as she tugs at her hair*) Do him in, Terry!
Choke a confession out of him! Do something to the little
creep before I murder him!

(MUM *appears through the french windows and stands looking at* KAREN. *She is wearing a black patch over her eye.*
HENRY *crosses to the cocktail cabinet while* TERRY *goes
to above the sofa.*)

MUM (*icily*) This happens to be my house, Karen, and there are

two things I won't tolerate guests doing in my house. One
is spitting, the other's shouting abuse at people. After all,
I've got certain standards to maintain. Excuse me. (*She
walks in front of* KAREN *and sits.*)

TOM (*staring at* MUM *as she moves in to* C.) What's up with
you? Lost your eyeball?

MUM It come out while I was bending over the bonfire, son.
(*To* KAREN.) You know, we girls wouldn't last two seconds,
if we set alight to ourselves. All that lingerie of Henry's
just went like that.
(KAREN *rises in a fury and crosses to french windows.*)

TOM Well, I'm off to bed.

MUM (*to* SHIRLEY) Keep out of sight when the police come,
Shirley. I don't want them to think I'm running a brothel.

TOM (*going upstage*) Good night, all.

MUM Kiss for Mum seeing it's her anniversary?
(TOM *grins as he wanders down to the sofa. He bends over
to kiss* MUM *and she swiftly puts an arm round his neck
and presses her mouth hungrily against his. It is a few
moments before* TOM *is able to break away.*)
(*To* SHIRLEY *with a twinkle.*) Follow that, dear, if you can.

TOM (*furiously, as he wipes his mouth with a handkerchief*)
God, you're disgusting at times. (*He goes out.*)

MUM (*having made herself comfortable again*) Yes, well I feel
better for that. Given me a bit of the old sparkle back.

TERRY Mum, the police will be arriving at any moment!

MUM Don't raise your voice, Terry, or Shirley here won't be
able to think of an excuse to slip upstairs. All right, Shirley. We'll be quiet. Take your time.
(TERRY *turns impatiently upstage while* KAREN *sits on the
L. arm of sofa. There is a short silence.*)

HENRY (*quietly*) We're not being fair——

MUM (*swiftly*) Shut up you!
(*After a moment or two* SHIRLEY *rises and starts to walk
to the door.*)

HENRY (*speaking kindly*) Just keep walking, Shirley. Out the front
door. I'll see you get your case.

SHIRLEY But I need him.

HENRY Only because you're in this house.

SHIRLEY No. I love him, and I've got his baby, you see.

MUM (*smoothing her dress*) Not very original, are you, dear?

SHIRLEY It doesn't show, I know.

MUM But it does.

SHIRLEY You knew?

MUM (*stretching her neck and feeling the front of it*) Up here it showed. Round here.

KAREN (*frowning*) He's never gone this far before.

HENRY I think we ought to make her leave.

MUM (*with narrowed eyes*) You know, it's about time you had treatment for your complaint, Henry. It's affecting your mind.

(TERRY *glances across at* MUM.)

SHIRLEY (*bravely*) You're the one who ought to walk out, Henry.

HENRY (*kindly as he sits in armchair* R.) I've nowhere to go, Shirley.

SHIRLEY Neither will I once my parents find out about the kid.

MUM (*with dignity*) Thank God, there are still some people left with Christian values. Not many of us, I admit; but a few. At least I know she comes from a decent family, so that's one worry I can cross off.

SHIRLEY (*hopefully*) Are you pleased about the baby, Mum?

MUM No, not really. I keep seeing your ears on him.

(SHIRLEY *gazes at* MUM's *back. She then turns and goes out.*) *With a brief glance over her shoulder.*) Walked out a bit different from last time, didn't she?

TERRY (*taking a few paces in*) Did you mean that about Henry needing treatment, Mum?

MUM Why?

TERRY Well, it's what he would get if he gave himself up.

MUM (*indignantly*) I'm not having no son of mine hauled up in front of a magistrate.

TERRY But what about me?

MUM You needn't be there neither.

KAREN He needn't?

MUM Not if he does his Mum a favour.

KAREN (*suspiciously*) What's the favour?

MUM Forget about Canada.

(KAREN *crosses to the french windows.*)

And don't ever turn round and say I never gives you a choice.

(*A defeated* TERRY *joins* KAREN.)

TERRY Let's do it, Karen. Let's tell her straight away : now, right now.

KAREN (*turning*) No, Terry, no.

TERRY But I'll never get into Canada with a pervert label stuck all over me, will I? Well, will I?

KAREN This is all so stupid. There must be a way out.

TERRY (*angrily*) Look, I'm not being convicted of stealing a girl's suspender belt; I'm not having people say I'm abnormal. I've got my pride.

KAREN But there's Shirley and Tom. They'll tell the truth. And there's the clothing. We'll tell the police about the burnt clothing.

TERRY (*forlornly as he sits* D.L.) I won't stand a chance; not if they haul me off to the station. Remember the last time?

KAREN (*quietly as she gazes at* TERRY) What is it, Terry? Are you just looking for an excuse to stay? Don't you want to go? Would you rather wait for her to forgive you? For what you did twenty odd years ago? And to hell with me and the children. Is that it? Have you just been kidding me along about Canada?

TERRY (*lamely*) No, but, Mum, she did say we'd be easing off on the housebuilding. Well, didn't she? And that's what was getting me down.

(KAREN *sits on the sofa and looks at* TERRY *before turning to gaze bitterly at* MUM.)

KAREN God, you've had a good anniversary, haven't you?

MUM (*cheerfully*) And it's not over yet.

TERRY All right, Mum. Get us out of it.

MUM What, so that Karen can give me the old two-fingers when I've done it, and rush home to pack? No, I now want an I.O.U. for five thousand two hundred and fifty quid.

(*She opens her evening bag and takes out pen and paper.*)

KAREN (*staring at* MUM) But that's Terry's money.

MUM It is : until I get the I.O.U.

KAREN But you gave it to Terry, told him to blew the lot.

MUM   I bet he's sorry he didn't take Mum's advice?

KAREN   (*with a helpless gesture*) Do as she says, Terry. Write it out.

MUM   No, I'd prefer it coming from you, Karen; seeing as how
you're the one who's got it stowed away.
(*There is silence while* TERRY *and* KAREN *stare at each
other.*)

TERRY   All right, write it out.

KAREN   (*taking up the pen*) Will ink do, Mum? Or do you want it
in blood?
(MUM *chuckles as* KAREN *starts to write the I.O.U. Suddenly two almighty screams of horror from* SHIRLEY *are
heard.* KAREN, TERRY *and* HENRY *rise in some alarm.* HENRY
goes into the hall.)

MUM   (*with a pained expression*) I do hope this isn't one of her
mannerisms. It's very off-putting.
(*Another scream is heard.*)

HENRY   (*coming D.C.*) Sounds as if it's coming from your room.

MUM   Oh, well, in that case, she probably came across my glass
eye. I left it on the pillow.

KAREN   You said you lost it in the bonfire.

MUM   Don't start confusing the issue, Karen. I've just told you,
I left it on my pillow.

TERRY   Have you signed that I.O.U. yet?

KAREN   (*still gazing at* MUM) What?
(*She sits and writes out the I.O.U. Another scream is heard.*)

MUM   Yes, it sounds as if finding it has given her a little shock.

HENRY   (*gazing at* MUM) You shouldn't have done that, Mum.

MUM   Well, dear, by rights she shouldn't really be in my bed,
should she? (*To* KAREN.) Done it yet, love?
(*As* KAREN *gives her the I.O.U.*)
Thank you. Very sweet of you.
(HENRY *crosses D.L. A very worried-looking* TOM *enters the
room as* MUM *puts the I.O.U. into her bag.*)

MUM   Still looking at my glass eye, is she?

TOM   (*troubled as he picks up the telephone and dials*) I think
it's given her a miscarriage.

KAREN   (*crossing to door*) Oh, no! She must be frightened out of
her wits.

MUM   (*to* TOM) What do you think you're doing?

TOM Phoning for an ambulance.

MUM (*crossing to the phone*) Here, give me that.

(MUM *takes the phone and* KAREN *comes downstage to listen.*)

MUM Police. (*Smiling sweetly.*) Oh, good evening. I wish to report a stolen car. No, it's my son's actually. We've been having a party here, and he was about to leave when he found his car wasn't where he parked it. (*Pause.*) Oh, hold on, please. (*Holding out the receiver.*) He wants name, address, registration number, etcetera.

(TERRY *turns upstage as he talks into the receiver.*)

See? Whoever pinched the car must have pinched the undies. Simple, don't you think? (*As* KAREN *crosses towards the door.*) Where do you think you're going?

KAREN (*angrily*) Somebody ought to be sitting with her.

(KAREN *goes out and* HENRY *sits* D.L.)

MUM It's taken her long enough to realise it. She's always got to be prodded, hasn't she? (*She rises.*)

TOM (*taking a few paces upstage*) Do you think I ought to go up?

MUM (*taking his arm and leading him to the sofa*) No, you're better down here.

TOM (*worried*) She'll be all right, will she, Mum? (*Sitting on the sofa.*)

MUM (*smiling kindly*) Of course she'll be all right.

TOM Seemed to be in a lot of pain.

(MUM *ruffles his hair before crossing to the cocktail cabinet.*)

MUM Not pain, dear. Discomfiture. Like hay-fever.

(*She opens the cabinet doors and the tune 'Auld Lang Syne' is heard tinkling merrily away.*)

TOM I'm glad she's stopped screaming.

MUM Yes, there doesn't seem to be much consideration there, does there? What will you have, Henry dear?

HENRY Brandy please, Mum.

MUM (*pouring out the brandy*) Tom?

TOM I don't know that I want anything.

MUM Do you good, son. You've had a shock.

(TERRY *replaces the receiver and sits* D.L.)

TERRY I'll have a brandy, too. And hurry up and stop that music, Mum.

MUM (*surveying the cabinet*) Yes, well, I think I'll have creme de menthe. (*Taking out the bottle and closing the doors, thus stopping the music.*) Don't you like the tune then?

TERRY It hardly goes with what's happening upstairs, Mum.

MUM (*handing* HENRY *a glass and then returning for two more glasses*) You can hardly blame a little musical-box for her up there going and getting herself pregnant, Terry.

TERRY It was Tom who put her that way.

MUM (*handing* TERRY *a glass*) No, I'm not having that. I'm not having Tom being the scapegoat.

TERRY He should have taken precautions.

MUM I expect he did. (*Handing* TOM *a glass.*) It must have been one of the others who didn't. I always say, if you have your fun, you must expect to pay for it.

HENRY (*quietly returns to the cocktail cabinet*) You never do, Mum.

(MUM *glances at* HENRY *with a momentarily sour expression before smiling.*)

MUM (*lightly*) Oh, go and get yourself a pair of knicks, dear. (*She picks up her glass and crosses to armchair* R.)

TERRY But it's true, Mum. You get off scot-free all the time. (MUM *smiles and gazes at* TERRY.)

MUM I'll be obliged if you will pick me up in your car at six o'clock sharp tomorrow morning, Terry.

TERRY (*staring at* MUM) Six o'clock?

MUM I want to start work on the office-block as soon as possible.

HENRY (*surprised*) What office block?

MUM You know that plot I bought close to the station a couple of years ago? Well, they want an office-block there. Didn't I tell you?

HENRY The last thing you said about the business was that we wouldn't be working so hard in the future.

MUM Ah, that was before you all upset me. But there are always compensations, dear. I'm turning us into a limited company; and I'm making you, Henry, and you, Tom, company directors. That means fat fees for you two from now on.

TERRY What about me, Mum?

MUM   (*softly*) I'm very annoyed with you, Terry.
       (KAREN *enters to above sofa table.*)
       (*sitting in armchair.*) Why aren't you still up there, Karen?

KAREN   She's not losing it. False alarm.
         (TOM *rises and goes upstage to R. of door.*)

MUM   The little devil. And to think I've been worrying myself
       sick about her. What's she doing now, then: having a
       good giggle at our expense?

KAREN   She's sobbing her heart out.

MUM   Of course she is. It's all part of the act.

KAREN   It's not an act! She's in a state, I tell you. You could have
         murdered that baby.

MUM   Hearing you talk anyone'd think I pushed her into a bath
       of hot gin.

TOM   (*turning*) Putting your glass eye on the pillow wasn't that
       much different, was it?

TERRY   (*rising*) You shouldn't have done that, Mum.

HENRY   No, you went too far, Mum.

KAREN   All evening you've been picking on her.

MUM   Listen to them. Just listen to them. Oh so innocent, oh so
       righteous, oh so moral. And yet not one of you stood up
       and said to me: No more, pack it in.

KAREN   We didn't know you'd gone upstairs.

MUM   (*rising*) Before, dear! Before! All evening according to you
       lot I've been playing with her as if she's mortar at the end
       of my trowel. Well, why didn't none of you face up to
       me, give me a clip, put me out? No, don't point the finger
       at me, 'cos it's a crooked one and it points right back to
       yourselves. (*She places her glass on the coffee table and
       turns to go upstage, having put her children in their place.*)

KAREN   Nuts!
         (MUM *is flabbergasted as she gapes at* KAREN.)

MUM   What did you say?

KAREN   I said nuts!

TERRY   You didn't show a scrap of feeling when you thought
         Shirley was having a miscarriage.

MUM   (*defensively as she crosses to* TERRY) Pardon me, I was
       very concerned.

TOM So concerned you thought it was like having a mild attack of hay fever.

MUM (*crossing towards* TOM) Because I knew she was coming it.

HENRY No, Mum. You were hoping she'd lose that baby.

MUM (*crossing to* HENRY *who rises*) What a terrible thing to say about your own mother. What kind of a woman do you think I am, for God's sake?
(HENRY *gives a withering grunt and turns upstage as* TOM *comes to* L. *of* MUM.)

TOM I'll tell you. You wouldn't have been content just knitting away during the French Revolution like the other hags. Oh, no. You'd have been up there working the guillotine yourself. And then you'd have gone round with your basket flogging the heads, three a tanner.
(MUM *crosses towards* TERRY *as* KAREN *joins* TOM.)

KAREN (*earnestly*) Tom, you've got to make her pay for what she did to Shirley tonight. She mustn't get away with it.

MUM Terry.

TERRY Not a scrap of feeling.
(TERRY *goes upstage and then quietly makes his way* D.R.)

TOM What do you suggest, Karen: sit her on top of the bonfire?

KAREN No, Tom. Just clear out of here. Without you lot to feed on, she'd starve and I want to see her starve. (*Crossing to* MUM.) I want to see her whole body shrivel. I want to see the cracks appear. I want to see the maggots get at her. Leave her, Tom. Leave her.

MUM My God, she's scummy green with envy, and all because—

KAREN Then it's tit for tat, isn't it? You want Shirley and me in hell because we got our men without having to throttle them first. (*Turning to* TOM.) Get out, Tom. Go to Shirley.

MUM He'll do no such thing.

TOM She won't want anything more to do with me, Karen: not after what I've put her through tonight. But I'll find my girl, don't you worry.

KAREN Tom! Your girl is waiting in the car.
(TOM *stares at* KAREN.)

TOM (*in disbelief*) She still wants me?

KAREN Yes. (*With a faint smile.*) She must be out of her mind, eh?

(KAREN *crosses to* TERRY.)

TOM She still wants me?

KAREN (*turning*) Yes!

TOM (*hardly believing his luck*) Mum's been beaten. My little Shirley can't be broken. (*Pointing to* MUM.) We've got her dangling at the end of a skewer at last. (*Crossing to* MUM.) Well, now I'm going to roast you. I am leaving you, dear. Don't forget to mention me in your will. (*He turns and goes upstage.*)

MUM You're not going nowhere.

TOM (*fervently as he turns*) Come and stop me; give me an excuse to push you through the roof.

MUM (*crossing to above sofa*) But when will I see you again?

TOM In hell. Plot 27.

MUM You'll never leave me.

TOM You're a bit slow on the uptake all of a sudden, darling. Haven't you been listening to the conversation? I'm leaving with Shirley, and I'm getting a special licence in the morning.

HENRY May I be your best man, Tom?

TOM You can be my best man with pleasure, Henry. In fact, if you like, you can be one of the bridesmaids.
(TOM *goes out. There is a short silence as* MUM's *venom starts to spill over.*)

MUM Do you think he'll come back?

HENRY (*soothingly*) Don't worry about it now.

MUM (*spitting out the words*) Will he come back, I said?

HENRY I shouldn't think so, Mum.
(MUM *slowly crosses to* KAREN.)

MUM It was you who goaded my Tommy into leaving me. You're like a cancer. From the moment you come into the family the filth started to spread.

TERRY Look, Mum, I know you're upset about losing Tom——

MUM And you was the one who brought her in. Well, I promise you, Terry, I'll have your skin for rags and I'll wipe them round the faces of your kids.
(TERRY, *moving out of danger, crosses to the piano.*)

KAREN (*staring at* MUM) God, he's your son.
(MUM *now feels she is in command again.*)

MUM   He's not a son. He's just slops. (*Sitting on the sofa.*) The
only thing he gives me is the shudders. Always has done.
Right from the start. No wonder he reminds me of his dad.
Him stuck up there on the piano. He was another wet
spaniel with the slobbers.
(KAREN *moves up to join* TERRY, *hoping that he has under-
stood what* MUM *has just said.*)

HENRY   (*to R. of sofa*) Now, now, Mum. You were very fond of
Dad.

MUM   Of course I was. After he'd been laid out.

TERRY   (*embarrassed*) You don't mean that, Mum, or we wouldn't
be remembering him tonight.

MUM   All been done to fool the gullible and everyone's so gullible, aren't they?
(HENRY *sit* D.R. *as* TERRY *comes down to* L. *of sofa.*)

TERRY   You've never felt anything for me?

MUM   Eh?

TERRY   Is that what you said?

MUM   (*defensively*) Yes, well if you didn't hear me first time
round, Terry——

TERRY   Is that what you said? I want to know.

KAREN   (*almost running the few paces to the sofa*) Yes, she did!
So it had nothing to do with shooting out her eye.

TERRY   (*to* MUM) It was the accident that turned you against me.

KAREN   No, no, no! She has never given a damn! You've got to
get that into your thick skull. To her you've always been
just a—just, just, a wet spaniel with the slobbers.

MUM   Pardon me, Karen——

KAREN   (*crossing towards* HENRY) No, I'm not having you sliding
out of this one. That's what she said, eh?

MUM   I was being facetious, dear.

KAREN   (*turning*) Nuts! (*Crossing to above sofa.*) Look, Terry, for
years, you've been waiting for her to show that she cares
for you. Well, God, I know how you feel because I've
been waiting for something like that from you; some little
sign to tell me I'm not just second best. If you felt like it,
you could give it me now, Terry. Well, surely my love's
better than nothing; and that's all you're going to get from
her. She'll just scoff the pickled onions, hand you the

empty jar and say 'aren't they lovely' as she breathes all over you.

MUM So we've got another ultimatum, have we?

KAREN (*moving right*) No, no, not at all. No, I'd be quite happy just to hear him say that he'll see less of you from now on.

MUM If you want my love, Terry, you'll do no such thing.

TERRY (*quietly*) I'm sorry about Tom, Mum. (*Glancing across at* KAREN.) Time we was pushing off, Karen. Your mum will start worrying. You know what she's like. (*He crosses to the door.*)

MUM (*rising and easing left*) Don't forget to pick me up at six o'clock tomorrow morning, Terry.

TERRY (*evenly*) I'll be too busy, Mum.

MUM Doing what?

TERRY (*looking at* KAREN) There's a lot to sort out if we're going to Canada.

(KAREN *spins round in wonderment.*)

MUM (*with a chuckle*) Canada, he says. As if it's just outside Wimbledon. (*Joining* TERRY.) Of course, this is typical of you, Terry. You wait till you're about to leave before telling me this news. Now, what I want——

TERRY (*angrily as he pushes her away*) It's finished, Mum! Forget it! (*Nodding to* KAREN.) Come on, Karen.

MUM (*as* TERRY *starts to go*) Terry!

(TERRY *goes and* KAREN *is so full of emotional relief that she can hardly speak.*)

KAREN (*half crying, half laughing in adoration*) He's an old twicer, isn't he? But he's beautiful with it. God, he's beautiful.

(*She crosses to the door, turns, desperately wants to say something but can't put her feelings into words. In the end she flings up her arms and shouts triumphantly.*) Yahoo!

(*And still crying and laughing she goes out.* MUM *leans on the table thoroughly beaten. After a few moments she looks across at* HENRY *sprawled out in the chair. He answers* MUM's *look of loathing with a wide smile.*)

HENRY (*kindly as he rises and crosses upstage*) Yes, well, I think I'll go upstairs, Mum; have my bath.

MUM   (*crossing to sofa*) Who was that mucky French artist who was always painting fat women getting in and out of baths?

HENRY   I don't know, Mum. Why?

MUM   (*contemptuously*) He'd have loved you.
(HENRY *looks at her and then smiles again.*)

HENRY   Good night, Mum.
(HENRY *goes and there is a short silence as* MUM *sits on the sofa and picks up her drink.*)

MUM   (*sourly*) I don't know. Kids. Who'd have 'em? They only do you in the end.

(*The* CURTAIN *slowly falls.*)

PROPERTY LIST

ACT I

Door shut
French windows shut
Window R. shut
Curtains open

Table (above sofa)
On it:
Telephone
Brass vase
Ashtray

Coffee table (below sofa)
On it:
Cigarette box (with cigarettes)
Lighter (practical)
Ashtray

Glass cabinet
Inside:
Mementoes and souvenirs including a nappy
On it:
Small mirror
China jug
Back-scratcher
Hanging on R. wall:
Two framed certificates
Two framed diplomas

Upright piano
On it:
Framed snapshots of children
Large framed photograph of Dad
Framed certificate
Three greetings cards

Wastepaper basket R. of piano

Cocktail cabinet
Inside:
Bottle of brandy (practical)

Bottle of creme de menthe
(practical)
Other bottles
Four brandy glasses
One liqueur glass
On it:
Brandy bottle with sufficient drink
for two glasses
Table lamp

Offstage
Flowers wrapped in cellophane
(HENRY)
Flowers wrapped in cellophane
(TERRY)
Flowers wrapped in cellophane
(KAREN)
Woman's magazine (HENRY)

In Hall
Raincoat (HENRY)

PERSONAL
SHIRLEY
Handbag containing mirror

TOM
Cigarette-lighter (practical)

TERRY
Wad of fivers
Car keys
Cigarette-lighter (practical)

KAREN
Coat
Handbag containing cigarettes and
matches
Shopping basket containing toys and
a pair of shoes

MUM
  Mink coat
  Spy glass at end of a length of
    ribbon

Handbag containing long business-
  type envelope
Gloves

ACT II

Door shut
Curtains closed

Strike
  Flowers on table
  Woman's magazine

Set
  Flowers in vase on sofa table
  Six champagne glasses on top of
    cocktail cabinet
  Brandy glass
  Saucer on top of piano
  Saucer on top of glass cabinet
  Saucer on top of coffee table

Offstage
  Two vases filled with flowers
    (HENRY)
  Tin of nuts (KAREN)
  Bottle of champagne with cork
    removed (TERRY)
  Broken champagne glass (HENRY)

PERSONAL
TOM
  Cigar
TERRY
  Handkerchief

ACT III

Door open
French windows open
French window curtains open

Strike
  Champagne glasses

Set
  MUM's evening bag containing pen
    and paper (Coffee table)

Offstage
  Long drawer filled with women's
    underwear (HENRY)

Two cardboard boxes filled with
  women's underwear (MUM)
Eye-patch (MUM)

SOUND EFFECTS
  Cars arriving and departing
  Musical-box rendering of Auld Lang
    Syne

The curtains are manually operated
  offstage

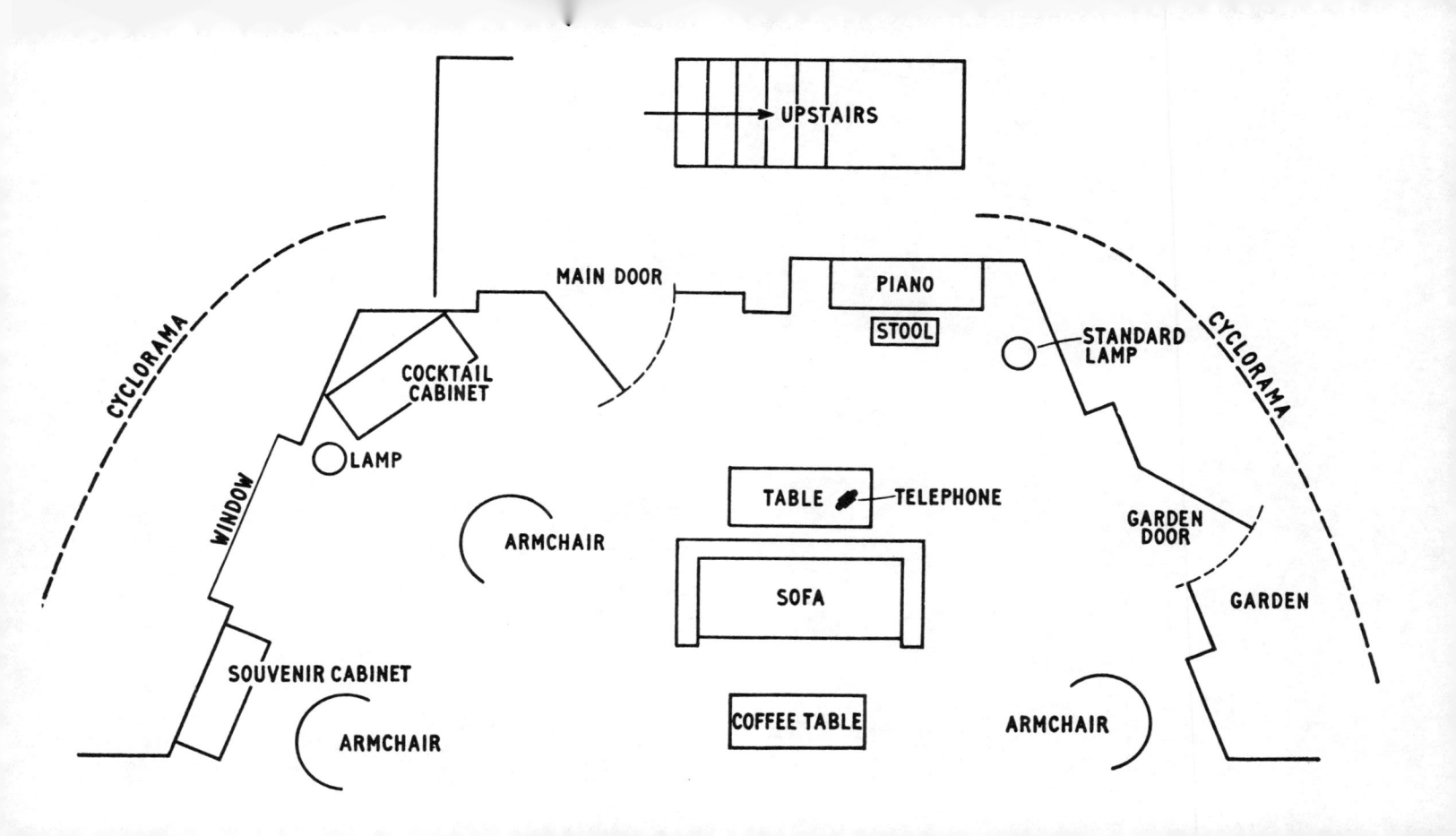

SOME PRESS OPINIONS OF THIS PLAY

The Anniversary by Bill MacIlwraith is a gnashing of teeth, a litany of abuse, a hymn of hate against, of all things, motherhood.

Its message is that in every mother there is a Medea yearning for a chance to murder her own children and that celebrating Mother's Day is equivalent to honouring Caligula. Fortunately it is also very funny. . . .
Milton Shulman—*The Evening Standard.*

If a proletarianly-minded Sade were to rewrite Sidney Howard's attack on mothers in that forgotten play, 'The Silver Cord', he might produce something like William MacIlwraith's *The Anniversary.* This is about a mother who gathers her family around her to commemorate her husband's death, and, with smug smiles and vile imagination, poisons and mutilates them one by one with the venom and the rack of her insatiable hatred. . . .

Mr. MacIlwraith regards her as odious, and the rest of the family as contemptible. The play is conceived in cruelty, and it is very, very funny. . . .
Harold Hobson—*The Sunday Times.*

As her younger son puts it: 'Mum's sense of humour wafts over us like poison gas.' Except that they haven't invented a gas more virulent than the Mum that Bill MacIlwraith has created in *The Anniversary.*

Like giant tentacles, her loving arms stretch out to members of her family to crush their spirit.

She knows her son's weaknesses and plays on them maliciously. Henry with his penchant for wearing Marks and Spencer clothes—women's clothes. Terry, turned into a human jellyfish by a guilt complex. Tom with his sexual indulgences. . . .

A remarkable first play with the hate-ridden humour always drawing a well-balanced mixture of gasps and guffaws. . . .
Jack Lewis—*Sunday Citizen.*

PRINTED IN GREAT BRITAIN BY
HOBBS THE PRINTERS LTD, TOTTON, HAMPSHIRE SO40 3WX

MADE IN ENGLAND